I AM NO
LONGER MYSELF
WITHOUT YOU

JONATHAN RUTHERFORD

I AM NO
LONGER MYSELF

without you

AN ANATOMY OF LOVE

Flamingo
An Imprint of HarperCollins*Publishers*

Flamingo
An Imprint of HarperCollins*Publishers*
77−85 Fulham Palace Road,
Hammersmith, London w6 8jb

Published by Flamingo 1999
1 3 5 7 9 8 6 4 2

ISBN 0 00 255917 X

Set in Garamond 3 by
Rowland Phototypesetting Ltd,
Bury St Edmunds, Suffolk

Printed and bound in Great Britain by
Clays Ltd, St Ives plc

1

SILENCE

And seeking we lose, discovering we conceal.
For we are still searching for our childhood.

MIROSLAV HOLUB

I

In my early twenties F moved into my bedsit, and we
bought a new bed that took up half the floor. To reach
the tiny cooker we had to squeeze between the bed and my
desk. Despite the small size of the room a sense of spacious-
ness came from the two windows which looked out onto an
unkempt garden. On occasion we would stand by one of
the windows and watch the trees, the tangle of plants in
the overgrown borders, the patchwork of gardens stretching
down the street. We cooked elaborate meals in that oven,
balancing saucepans on the two rings, washing up in the
small circular sink. We took it in turns to work at my desk,
the desk I still use, which I had bought some years before
for £10, its oak veneer splintered along the edges. There
were bare boards on the floor which had been sanded down
and varnished. For heating we had a paraffin heater. I forget

what pictures we hung on the walls. F and I had only recently met when I moved to London. A friend of mine who was returning to the North offered me his bedsit and I spent several days painting the room before moving in. I had slept on the floor and had woken in the middle of the first night and wondered where I was. I lay awake in the dark, smelt the fresh gloss paint on the skirting boards and recalled a time before, crossing the North Sea on a ferry, sleeping on the packed deck, waking, sitting up, staring around me, feeling entirely lost and disorientated. As my eyes had grown accustomed to the dark, and the shapes of people appeared –slumped in chairs, talking quietly in groups or stumbling over prostrate bodies – my fear subsided. As a faint light revealed the landlord's cheap, brightly painted furniture I felt once again this disquieting solitude.

We lived in this room for two years and that was eighteen years ago. It was the beginning of our life together and so it is the beginning of this story. It is a narrative about myself. But it is also, more generally, about the relationships and feelings of men. It turns inward to the life of home and intimacy, and to the words we use to define ourselves. And it is a story about the silence which surrounds men's love and their relationships with women. To write about men's love and relationships is like entering an uncharted territory and inventing its geography. I must attempt to map its contours, define the gradations of the hills, the sharp dip of valleys, describe the climate and vegetation, put words to places whose histories I don't fully comprehend. I'm not sure what I will find, and I'm not sure what I'll say.

I can remember exactly when I first knew that I was in love with F. It was October, shortly after she had moved in. We visited Chichester and walked across a field towards the town. It was early evening, and we stopped to look at the shapes of the roof tops against the darkening blue sky. The autumn yellow of the sun lit the steeple of a church and reflected off the glass block of an office building. We had left the road and climbed a stile, jumping down into the coarse grass. There were a few cows who were ruminating or lying on the soft, damp earth. We had spent the summer taking day trips to the sea and countryside, and this was to be our final outing. Chichester had proved to be an uninteresting town, yet looking at its unprepossessing skyline, I felt my life had changed irrevocably. I had given up my solitude. This moment belonged to both of us, but not to each alone. While I remained 'I', a significant part of myself had become 'we'. I was not overwhelmed with transcendent joy. There was no flood of romantic dreaming. I experienced hope and a sense of my life beginning, pleasure that I had been released from the confinement of myself, anxiety at this other life now incorporated into my own.

When men fall in love we surrender our solitude and relinquish our masquerade of self-sufficiency. A new story of our lives is waiting to begin; a recognition that 'I am no longer myself without you'. The paradox of love is that we discover a new sense of self in the moment we lose our self to another person. Men avoid this paradox, because love must develop into a relationship – a negotiation of give and take, autonomy and dependency – and faced with such a prospect we have traditionally retreated and recouped some of our solitude. Intimacy changes the boundaries of our self and we become ambivalent about who we are and what we want, and in this equivocation lies apprehension. We are unsure how to respond. Masculinity – an identity rooted in the language of work and public life – has left men unskilled in the necessary words of feeling, empathy and love.

Love is a fugacious word. Rounded and comfortable, it lifts the tongue and fills the back of the throat, before slipping beyond reach as the sound is exhaled from the mouth. Yet the word eludes meaning. Love teeters on the edge of the unknown beyond which it becomes almost impossible to speak. It moves us beyond words. We speak about love when we define our longing and desire and yet we fall into silence when we attempt to speak about it in the present. I fumble for words, my mind's eye searching for that thought or that feeling to which I can attach the right sound, make it sound right, let it appear to emanate from inside myself. I attempt to speak about love in the way many men can about politics or sport, with passion and intensity. But in times of trouble the words just buckle and fold and disappear, and I am thrown back on foolish clichés which slide across my palate. While I may have everything to say, I say nothing or I say very little.

We use words to represent our feelings and to communicate them to others. What we feel and think about ourselves is subject to available vocabularies. But supposing the vocabularies I need are not there. Suppose I want to talk about certain feelings I have – for example, the disquiet I experience in my dependency on others. The words might not be there for me to use, yet I know the feeling is real. There is something more, an excess of world over word. Perhaps this is the case for men. Our feelings can be enacted, lived, dreamed and embodied. We attempt to represent them in music, in literature and in art, but they remain always just beyond our understanding. When I began writing this book I tried to recall all the films I'd watched, the art I'd seen and the books I'd read about men in love. I went to galleries and bookshops and leafed through novels and biographies. I wrote down lists of famous writers. I wanted to know what other men had written about love, and how they had expressed themselves.

I have watched John Huston's film adaptation of Joyce's story *The Dead* several times. I watched it again for the final scene. Greta and Gabriel have entered a Dublin hotel room. They are spending the night in the city after celebrating New Year's Eve with Gabriel's aunts and a circle of friends. Greta is melancholy and her husband asks her what is wrong: 'Tell me, I think I know what the matter is. Do I know?' She tells him that a song sung that evening by a member of their party had reminded her of a boy she had known when she was a young girl living with her grandmother in Galway. His name was Billy Furey. 'He was very delicate; such eyes, big dark eyes.' Gabriel is momentarily gripped by jealousy. But his wife explains that Billy Furey died when he was only seventeen. 'What was it he died of?' he asks. She begins to cry. 'I think he died from me.' She had been leaving her grandmother's house for a convent school in Dublin. The boy had been ill for a number of months. She wrote and told him of her departure and the night before she left, while she was packing. Billy Furey left his sick bed to visit her. He threw gravel up to her window. She slipped out of the house and found the boy, poorly dressed, shivering in the rain. She implored him to go home before he caught his death. He refused to leave and told her he had no wish to live without her. Eventually he relented and returned home. A week after her arrival in Dublin he died.

Overcome with the grief of this memory, Greta collapses onto the bed, sobbing. She buries her face in a pillow and falls asleep. Gabriel sits beside her. He tentatively strokes his wife's hair. At a loss to know what to do or feel, he crosses to the window and looks outside. It is snowing. He thinks to himself: 'How poor a part I've played in your life. It's almost as though I'm not your husband and we've never lived together as man and wife.' He recalls their evening spent with his elderly aunt, Julia. He feels momentarily the proximity of Julia's death and imagines his own mourning; his 'casting around for words of consolation only to find lame and useless ones'. He is shaken by the depth of his wife's lament for Billy Furey, and by the actions of the boy who did not wish to live without her. He knows that this is love and it is something that he has never felt for a woman. There is something in the world that he is unable to speak of, and soon death will come for him and his time will be over.

I have a battered copy of *Dubliners*, James Joyce's short stories. Opening it I saw my brother's name on the inside cover. It was his school text book and he had written his name in red biro across the spine, but the first and the last letters of his surname were in blue and they have faded –

UTHERFOR. I read James Joyce's original story and compare it to the film. It differs to an important degree. Gabriel contemplates his wife's sleeping form and he is drawn to the vast hosts of the dead. His thoughts turn to his mortality, he looks inside himself and he sees the ethereal quality of his love reaching across the landscape of Ireland, falling with the snow, as vast and as amorphous as the dark night he looks out on. Tears gather in his eyes. He finds solace in the thought of death, and in the transmutation of his body into the impalpable world of nothingness. There is something religious in the way Gabriel loves. He uses words to distance himself from his feelings and his body. I am reminded of the asceticism of Christ, his male body martyred in the name of his love, his pain an erotic depiction of the union of ecstasy and death. Gabriel cannot express himself to his wife; instead he casts his love like a mantle across the world. It enhances everything, but no one in particular.

Men have frequently expressed their love in these abstracted terms, loving humanity and life in general. Or they have fallen in love with the idea of love, imbuing women with the transcendent qualities of beauty and innocence. Men have loved in chivalrous oblation to their chosen one and, as in the decrees of knightly courtship, have sacrificed themselves in the name of love. When a man worships his beloved there is no relationship. She remains a figment of his imagination. In love, women are annulled by men. The philosopher Immanuel Kant wrote: 'Sexual love makes of the loved person an object of appetite; as soon as the appetite has been stilled the person is cast aside as one casts away a lemon which has been sucked dry.' A man might sacrifice his life for his country, merge himself with the transcendental symbols of race and nation, but he will not easily give his emotions to a lover. We remain reluctant to give away too much of ourselves to women.

The more I read men writing on love, the greater the sense I have of their plight. When men write about love they communicate a state of bereavement. They preserve their solitariness. Shelley's 'Dedication' at the beginning of his epic poem, *The Revolt of Islam*, is addressed to Mary Shelley, his lifelong companion and lover. It expresses his loneliness, his longing for a friend and lover and his gratitude. 'Aught but a lifeless clod, until revived by thee'. He measures his love by her absence. She is the bearer of his life and love, and without her he is nothing. The language of romantic love and relationships belongs to women. In the intimate life of the emotions and the body, women frequently speak on behalf of men: wives for husbands, mothers for sons, girlfriends for boyfriends. Men doubt their ability to love. I used to read W. H. Auden when I was younger and remember his poem 'Lullaby' and the poignant lines, 'Lay your sleeping head, my love, / Human on my faithless arm.' They reveal a scepticism about the poet's own capacity to love. It is as if the one he holds contains all the feelings of goodness and empathy and concern that he – 'faithless' – lacks. It is this lack that propels men's need of women. Marcel Proust, compelled by the death of his mother to write *Remembrance of Things Past*, began his voyage into memory with the sentence: 'For a long time I used to go to bed early.' Here he lies, a small, remorseful child anticipating the goodnight kiss of his mother. Neither asleep nor awake, he longs for her to remain with him through the coming 'sad hours of darkness'. Proust longed for maternal love. The nineteenth-century French novelist Stendhal longed for sexual love. He wrote his famous treatise *Love* out of unrequited passion for Mathilde Viscontini Dembowski. She neither loved nor understood him, but he persisted, humiliating himself in his attempts to win her affections. His imagination turned her into his obsession:

> Leave a love with his thoughts for twenty-four hours, and this is what will happen. 'At the salt mines of Salzburg, they throw a leafless wintry bough into one of the abandoned workings. Two or three months later they pull it out covered with a shining deposit of crystals. The smallest twig, no bigger than a tom-tit's claw, is studded with a galaxy of scintillating diamonds. The original branch is no longer recognisable.'

And nor was the hapless Mathilde.

Without women men are bereft; they lose the stories of their lives. They are unable to reflect upon themselves and their actions, and self-understanding escapes them. Men have dominated intellectual life as thinkers, writers, scientists and artists. But the language they have used has been designed to act upon and change the world, to dissect and analyse, not to reflect and intuit. Men have located the object of their inquiry somewhere beyond themselves and fashioned themselves into the detached observer, the disinterested scientist and the dispassionate critic. Men have used their intelligence to promote their separateness from others rather than to recognize their interdependence. They have used knowledge as a form of power over other people, in particular over women. Biology, theology, philosophy, psychiatry, psychoanalysis, medicine, the physical sciences, anthropology, literature – each discipline in its time has legitimized the inferiority of women, who have been classified and categorized as having smaller brains, a lack of rational intellect, oversexualized bodies, a mental predilection for hysteria, a lower order of spirituality, sentimentality, shorter attention spans and mental flightiness. The word 'epistemology' refers to the theory of knowledge. It was coined by a Scottish professor, James Frederick Ferrier. On Monday 17 November 1862 Elizabeth Garrett, a young medical student at St Andrews University, tried to enter a lecture theatre in order to attend a talk on chemistry and thus challenged the male dominance of the Scottish education system. It was Professor Ferrier who blocked her path and demanded she turn back, leaving her with little choice but to submit to his authority. Knowledge and language belonged to men but, used as a form of power, they have diminished self-understanding.

Men have used language in an instrumental way to separate ourselves from our own feelings. We have allowed women to voice our emotions. This is why men abandoned by women despair – they no longer know who they are. I think this is what Raymond Carver is trying to say in his short story *Blackbird Pie*. He describes a couple whose children have grown up, and who have moved to the country. The man enjoys the solitude, but his wife does not. He admits her discontent to himself, but makes no attempt to improve their situation. One night an envelope is pushed beneath the door of his room. Inside is a letter. It begins: 'It's been such a long time now since we've talked. I mean really *talked.*' She wants to leave him. He refuses to believe that the letter has been written by his wife; he opens the door of his room and looks down the corridor. Everything is as it should be and yet he feels suddenly afraid. Uneasy, he returns to his room and closes the door. He opens it for a second time and he hears a murmuring downstairs and the receiver of the telephone being replaced. He feels panic. He steps down the corridor hoping to hear the reassuring click of knitting needles. Instead he hears the sound of a door opening and closing quietly. Though his impulse is to investigate, he instead returns to his room, his heart racing. He picks up the letter and stares at the pages, snatching lines at random. When he hears the front door close he drops the pages and hurries to the living room. His wife is not in the house. The porch light is on and her suitcase stands on the porch outside.

Several days later the husband is going through his wife's belongings. He is packing to move and trying to decide which possessions of hers to take and which to discard. He knows now that she will never come back and that he may never see her again. He is still bewildered. He knows there is something 'far more' to this affair than his wife's simple departure:

You could say that my history has left me. Or that I'm having to go on *without* history. Or that history will now have to do without me – unless my wife writes more letters, or tells a friend who keeps a diary, say. Then years later, someone can look back on this time, interpret it according to the record, its scraps and tirades, its silences and innuendoes. That's when it dawns on me that autobiography is the poor man's history. And that I am saying goodbye to history. Goodbye my darling.

The husband in *Blackbird Pie* is sedentary, appearing unmindful of his wife. His life is governed by fear and selfishness. He feels that he cannot be himself in his relationship with her. He wants her to remain just beyond him, neither to move away from him, nor to come too close: to sit with her knitting, a comforting presence he can control. Like Gabriel in *The Dead*, the husband in Carver's story cannot tell his wife what he feels about himself and about her. Instead he tries to manage her. When she leaves he is lost for anything to say and his world begins to collapse. The hint of misanthropy which surrounds both men is echoed in Proust's lament for Albertine in *Remembrance of Things Past*: 'I knew now that I was in love with Albertine, but alas! I didn't trouble to let her know it . . . the declaration of my passion to the one I loved no longer seemed to be one of the vital and necessary stages of love. And love itself seemed no longer an external reality, but only a subjective pleasure.' Men's love is a pursuit through others of all they feel they have lost and cannot speak of. It is why they speak of it as a bereavement. That is the nature of love – the desire to achieve a sense of completeness through unity with another. Only when men fall in love with women, they fall in love with that part of themselves that is missing. Men want love because we long to be offered a semblance of ourselves. In love a man is held captive not by a woman, but by his need to be loved by her. He longs for her, he needs her to embrace him and fill him with her love, but when she desires something for herself, or when she withdraws from him emotionally, she exposes the absence in himself. He feels numbed and lifeless, and only she can revive him. He cannot find the words to speak of the emptiness and fear her absence induces in him. He is no longer himself without her. Love tyrannizes him.

Men have colluded in a masquerade of silence around their emotional dependency on women, their loud self-assurance, nothing more than a brittle patina. In truth, men are unsure what to do about themselves and what to do about women. Or rather they are unsure what to do about their need of women. Men have celebrated being alone in order to imagine themselves free of women, free from their vulnerability. In the past we have taken pleasure in our 'male only' cultures: the army, public schools, trade unions, political parties, banking and commerce, working men's clubs, gentlemen's clubs and pubs. The history of the British and their class system is a history of sexual apartheid in which men and women existed in separate spheres. Society has sustained and been sustained by a language of opposites which privileges the masculine term over the feminine: active and passive, rational and emotional, hard and soft, culture and nature, the sun and the moon, the mind and the body. It is a language whose descriptive vocabulary has given men prominence: the history of mankind, fellow countrymen, forefathers, masterful, God the Father, yours fraternally, man, amen. A plethora of words, a confident, assured language in service to men's authority which has been guaranteed by their monopoly of the public world of work and politics. In contrast their confused and tentative understanding of love and intimacy has been concealed in the privacy of the home. Today these old boundaries between the public and the private are breaking up and the culture of silence that has surrounded men's feelings – once portrayed as a sign of sexual magnetism and authority – has lost its allure. In spite of our command over language, when it comes to speaking about love, words fail us.

II

Next-door to our bedsit was a room not much larger than a cupboard. For a while Michael lived there; his groans of anguish used to wake us in the night. His room was filthy and littered with old food and empty beer cans. His clothes smelt, and his eyes were half-hidden by a face swollen from drink. A self-educated, literary man in his late thirties, he would catch me on the stairs and subject me to intense monologues. He used to look at me fiercely, his breath stinking of alcohol, and tell me his stories in a bitter monotone. I could never get away once he started talking. He told me he had once been in love. He had lived with a woman in a semi-detached house somewhere in the suburbs, and had a good job. He had given it all up because he could not cope with love. He had left her. He scoffed when he told me this, and I didn't know whether to believe him. He always ended his stories with the question 'What do you want?' For him this was the key to life, and he believed it would always elude him. 'You see,' he'd say, 'that's my problem. I don't know.'

Michael disappeared that winter. The garden was covered with snow. No one went into it, even in the summer, but that morning there were footprints leading from the house to the garden fence. Not shoe prints but bare feet. Outside our door the hallway was full of police. The man in the cupboard was on the run and had jumped out of his open window, half naked and shoeless. They caught him making his escape down the road.

At the time I wondered where Michael had intended to go. He had spent years wandering from one sleazy bedsit to another and had few friends. Though his mother lived only a few miles away, I doubted he was heading in her direction. He had simply run for his life and I don't think he gave a thought to where he was going. He was compelled to keep moving. That is what men do, he once told me. They pursue life. In both a metaphorical and a literal sense, men take to the road in search of their identities. They are uneasy about home, with its intimations of femininity and its constricting relationships. Generally young men do not daydream about a settled, domestic existence; instead they choose stories of travel, action and adventure. In their youth they leave behind their mothers and embark on voyages of discovery in search of themselves. The boy leaving home to seek his fortune is one of the oldest of all stories. He changes. He finds wisdom, kills his enemy, finds a wife, becomes rich and gains status and authority. When he returns, he has become a man.

When I was a boy, adventure stories mapped the geography of my desire: the sands tramped by the foreign legion, the seas sailed by plucky young English midshipmen, the veld of southern Africa, the islands, shipwrecks and pirates of England's maritime history. I escaped and travelled to every distant corner of the globe without leaving the confines of my bedroom. I had no fear of being lost or abandoned. I lived periodically in deserts, and as a castaway on tropical islands, my desire transmogrified into heroic feats of survival. I had created a dream world entirely my own, full of angels and demons and mythical beings. In later years I was captivated by the frontier spirit of the Beat generation – Jack Kerouac, Allen Ginsberg and Neil Cassidy, who headed across America demonstrating their rejection of the Cold War and 1950s white suburbia. The road was their metaphor for masculine freedom and self-expression, exemplified by Robert Frank's photograph *US 285, New Mexico*, an infinite road heading off into a limitless future. Kerouac, with his compulsion to travel without stopping, was the personification of mobility: 'somewhere along the line I knew there'd be girls, visions, everything; somewhere along the line the pearl would be handed me.' It never was. Kerouac ended his life in his mother's house, where he died a drunk, defeated by the impossibility of his longing.

Kerouac wanted the simple things in life – marriage, possibly children. He was old fashioned at heart. He craved love but never knew how to ask for it. He believed he'd find it over the next hill, in the next town, on the next journey. In my own youth I could see none of this hopeless-

16

ness because I was seduced by his poetry and the romanticism of his adventurous life. I dreamed of pursuing my life in the way that Kerouac had his. It never occurred to me that if I did so, I might end up running away from it. Kerouac pursued life because he felt he did not have it. The stories men write and tell each other – in literature, poetry, films, television programmes – provide us with the words and images of masculinity, giving us the means to define ourselves. Like the adventure stories of my boyhood, Kerouac's narrative offered me an opportunity to escape from the confinement of my upbringing. If I now return to the imaginary islands and deserts and roads of my boyhood and youth, it is to excavate these stories and undo them from the inside. I want to unpick the seam of their narratives and discover Kerouac's pearl – the silence I think I may find at their heart.

In recent years a new narrative of masculinity has emerged, which contradicts the conventional stories of ambition and worldly success. It is about men's feelings. Demand has increased for popular psychology books which focus on men's problems in communicating their feelings to others. Claude Steiner confesses in *Emotional Literacy*: 'I would say that many of the things I did were insensitive and hurtful to the people in my life . . . Looking back I see myself as someone who had infatuations but no real attachments, who had little respect, regret or guilt when it came to the way I treated others.' Some scientists are claiming that men's difficulties in empathizing with others is caused by their genetic makeup. Explanations are reduced to a crude form of Darwinism: men have spent thousands of years hunting and fighting in wars and gain some advantage by lacking the qualities of empathy and concern. It is an argument which assumes masculinity is a fixed and unchanging identity. I don't believe that our biology is our destiny. For me the distinctive problems men have in their relationships and in expressing their feelings are the consequences of our history and culture. There is no better illustration of this than Daniel Defoe's *Robinson Crusoe*. It was one of the first books I was given as a child. The writing was difficult and reading it lacked pleasure – yet it is memorable because its narrative defined all the subsequent adventure stories I read in my boyhood. It is a story about the making of modern masculinity. It provides an explanation for men's struggle with their feelings. It shows us what has made us into the men we are today.

Shipwrecked on a slaving expedition to Africa, Robinson Crusoe transforms the uninhabited island into his 'little kingdom'. He orders time and space, builds his fortress home, domesticates animals, produces candles, clay pots and plates, and after three years cultivates his field of barley and rice and earthen vessels for baking bread. It is an idyll without the complicating presence of women. He suppresses his emotional response to events in favour of rational explanation. His scientific observations and careful dissection and classification of experience distance him from the compromising enigma of his feelings.

He decides to write a journal, but delays starting it. When he does begin, he chooses to describe events retrospectively. He explains that if he had begun his journal immediately on being shipwrecked, 'I must have said thus: Sept.

30th. After I had escaped drowning . . . I ran about the shore, wringing my hands and beating my head and face, exclaiming at my misery, and crying out, I was undone, undone.' With the trauma behind him, he can exert a greater control over his feelings and master his words. His command of his emotions is projected onto his command of the island's resources. He is lord of the whole manor. There are no rivals, no competition, nobody to dispute his omnipotence. He is utterly alone, but he reflects on the benefits of his isolation. He has nothing to covet and nobody to lust after. Everything he enjoys he has made himself, for himself alone. It is a moment of personal triumph. But it also marks his downfall.

'One day, about noon, going towards my boat, I was exceedingly surprised with the print of a man's naked foot on the shore, which was very plain to be seen in the sand.' After fifteen years his self-made world is shattered. He cannot conceive of the existence of someone other than himself. He is haunted. He begins to imagine – hope against hope – that the footprint is a 'mere chimera of my own'. To no avail. Crusoe, the king of all that he knows, is almost driven mad by his terror of this unknowable print in the sand. He sleeps fitfully, dreams of the pleasures of murder and suffers lurid nightmares. The only significant emotion in the book is Crusoe's dread of being swallowed up by the unknown. War must be declared, both on himself for mastery of his emotions and against this nameless other who threatens his existence; either he devours or he will be devoured.

After twenty-four years alone on his island and nine years under the threatening shadow of this footprint, Crusoe

finally confronts the source of his dread and saves Friday
from being killed in a sacrificial ritual. His solitude is over.
But he is incapable of forming a relationship with Friday.
He fashions Friday into a simulacrum of himself – not a
threatening unknown nor an independent-minded individual, but a mimicry. He teaches him English – 'I . . .
taught him to say Master'. And like Crusoe's parrot, Friday's
language is a copy of Crusoe's own imperial identity – 'Yes,
master' to Crusoe's 'No, Friday.' After all the threat and
the terror, there is nobody to fear. *Robinson Crusoe* inaugur-
ates the story of the man who lives in the world as if it is
uninhabited.

Published in 1719, *Robinson Crusoe* is arguably the first
novel of modern England. Crusoe represents the exemplary
man of an increasingly confident middle-class society whose
principle of freedom lies in the unfettered pursuit of profit.
In such a culture the ideal man is the man who is alone,
unconstrained by his emotional need of women, or by concern for the lives of others. For Robinson Crusoe reason is
the font of truth and freedom. Defoe turns Crusoe's island
into an allegorical setting where his hero must confront his
irrational fears about his body, his feelings, his sexuality,
women and 'savages'. Crusoe imposes his rational order and
language on the island and turns it into a solipsistic world in
which other people are reduced to things, and relationships
become instrumental. But he is left with the anxiety that
the fear he has repressed lies beneath the surface of things,
ready to erupt into life and consume him. To keep order,
he must cultivate a manliness and master himself through
strenuous activity.

The story of Robinson Crusoe became an ideal vehicle for the imperial spirit of late Victorian England. Its story of manly self-sufficiency and survival provided a model for countless boys' adventure stories, eulogizing the exploits of Britain's empire-builders. Their boy heroes treated the empire like a vast playground, glorying in violence, and championing the team spirit and chauvinism of the public schools. 'The Englishman's idea is that the world is ruled by character, by will,' wrote the Hungarian anglophile Emil Reich in *Success Among Nations* in 1904. 'From the very earliest childhood,' he continued, 'the English boy is subjected to methodical will-culture; he is soon trained to suppress to the uttermost all external signs of emotion.' Out of this culture of asceticism emerged a form of imperial manliness which gained renown for its stiff upper lip, its masterly control over world affairs and its incomprehension of women and personal feeling. This is the manliness that we have inherited – a product not simply of our genetic makeup but of our history of empire, our relationships to women, and our functions within the newly emerging economic order of capitalism. This is the history of masculinity I inherited and it was a vital ingredient in shaping my language and identity. It determined the words I would use to describe who I was, and it gave form to the idiom of my life and relationships.

At the age of eight I was returning home from school one afternoon when, walking past the newsagents, I saw the *Victor* comic for boys slotted into a rack next to the door. On the cover was a wounded, bedraggled British Tommy, heroically struggling to fire his field gun at a group of advancing German Panzers. Around him were sprawled his dead companions. I recall being intensely attracted to this image and at that moment *Victor* became a part of my boyhood. The stories were pared down to the essentials of manly action. Characters like Captain Hurricane were cardboard cut-outs whose function was to carry the action and violence to its inevitable conclusion – a bloody pasting for 'Jerry'. Exclamations, grunts and inexplicable noises indicated the brute appeal of the male body. *Victor* depicted a manliness besotted with self-sacrifice and athleticism. But the enduring images in action and adventure stories of the wounded male body, shot up, filled with arrows, starved, beaten and tortured, gives another, contradictory account of the troubled relationship men have with their bodies. The renowned understatement and personal reserve of the hero as he is faced with danger – chin up, don't let the side down – cultivates an imperviousness to fear. His self-denial of his feelings transforms his wounds. He is a spectacle of righteous suffering, a martyr to his own pain. His emotional need is sublimated into his willingness to sacrifice his life for his country. Meaningless, catastrophic death is transformed into an eternal heroism, his short life into immortality. This celebration of death and suffering, the refusal to contemplate or be still, suggest that these stories of manliness involve a compulsion in men to elude their feelings and escape their own bodies.

Robert Falcon Scott's doomed expedition to the South Pole in 1911 was one of the last great examples of this kind of English adventure. Pitched against the unendurable, Scott played the part of the imperial hero in the vast white solitude of ice. Eleven miles from One Ton camp Scott and his four companions were caught in a storm which lasted for four days. Knowing they were about to die he composed a series of final letters. In one, addressed to his friend, the playwright Sir James Barrie, he wrote: 'we are in a desperate state, feet frozen, etc. No fuel and a long way from food, but it would do your heart good to be in our tent, to hear our cheery songs.' In another letter, addressed to the British public, he apologized for his failure. 'Had we lived,' he wrote, 'I should have had a tale to tell of the hardihood, endurance and courage of my companions which would have stirred the heart of Englishmen. These rough notes and our dead bodies must tell the tale.' This was how an Englishman should die, a willing accomplice to the rules of the game: his death should be free from the rictus and terror of personal annihilation, or the desperate pleading for a mother. And yet there is a frisson of anxiety. For Scott, the approach of death in the Antarctic brought with it a contemplation of his manliness. He wrote to his wife about his concern for his son: 'Above all, he must guard and you must guard him against indolence. Make him a strenuous man. I had to force myself into being strenuous, as you know – had always an inclination to be idle.' He ends his letter: 'What lots and lots I could tell you of this journey. How much better has it been than lounging in too great a comfort at home.' The loneliness of his frozen, emaciated death thousands of miles away from home confirmed him in his manhood. Yet the icy wastes of the Antarctic proved easier to confront than a deeper fear, closer to home – a life of domesticity with his wife and son. What the hero fears more than his enemy

and the hostile terrain he must journey across are those close
to him who want his love.

The stories of my boyhood transported me into an
imaginary world of manly solitude. They taught me a language of self-possession which, I imagined, would galvanize
me into independence. As a man I would step out into the
world, alone, with nothing to fear or be mindful of. I had
grown up in a middle-class society where emotions were
coded in order that they could be denied, or taken back
at a later date. The untempered expression of feelings –
tantamount to making a scene – was not good manners.
Neatly trimmed privet hedges and angled flower borders
were like totems warding off the outside world and sanctify-
ing the proper order within. Any emotional outburst –
antagonism, conflict, despair – was to be contained behind
closed doors. Nothing was to pass the obstinately patrolled
border between feelings and words. They were kept apart,
and in the silence which existed between people emotions
remained nebulous, confined to the kitchens and the bed-
rooms of children. In my youth I turned away from my
family. I had wanted my parents on their knees. I sought
release from the grip of their own fear of the world. For
their part they could make no reply to my intransigence. I
wanted to put my family behind me and make my own
way in life. My adventures would not take place in Africa,
or the Antarctic. The boundaries I wanted to cross were not
national or geographical but class and cultural. It was the
mid 1970s and there was still a strong and vibrant counter
culture. When I was nineteen, I spent the summer working
on a small community newspaper in north Lambeth,

London, before going to university. It was run by a group squatting in an old shop in Blackfriars, where local communities were hard pressed by property speculation and commercial redevelopment. I wanted to live what appeared to be a carefree existence. In the squat's messy kitchen, which looked out onto a high brick wall, they would hold collective meetings at eleven o'clock in the morning, smoking and drinking tea. Involuntarily, I was always discomfited by the casual, nonchalant way in which they eased themselves into daily activity.

I began university in the autumn. The clear delineation of its red-brick buildings and the neat squares of campus life echoed the suburban geography of my childhood from which I had longed to escape. In the summer of my first year I left. I had met a women called C who lived on a large estate on the edge of the city. She, along with a group of other tenants, was building an adventure playground on a piece of waste ground. Local firms were cajoled into making donations and the post office persuaded to part with a dozen telegraph poles. The local industrial estate was scoured for old timber, and materials were salvaged from skips. A complex structure of wooden poles and beams grew from the ground, a matrix of walkways, swings and tunnels. Adults and children hammered and roped the warren, arguing about the course of its development and the merit of one design over another. I lived close by and began working there.

C had three children. The first time I walked through her back door I was taken aback by the poverty. In the small kitchen was a dirty stove, upon which stood a large

chip pan. A vague smell of old chip fat and unwashed clothes
lingered. Outside, the garden was a turmoil of broken toys,
old bikes and junk. An apple tree stood in its centre, still
alive, blossoming.

'Want some apples?' said her younger son to me.

'There aren't any,' I replied.

'Smart mush!'

In the dining room stood a couple of chairs and a solid
table strewn with old copies of the local newspaper. An ash
tray was pushed to the edge, brimming with cigarette butts
and ash. It was perilously close to falling off. The wallpaper
was peeling and torn; threadbare rugs partially covered the
grey linoleum floor. When C came into the room I smiled
and said hello and she said, 'Ah! Hello.'

I had spoken to C once or twice before. She was in her
late forties. Her hair was greying and messy. She had a snub
nose and wore glasses. She dressed in whatever clothes came
her way, which gave her an unconventional appearance. She
was outspoken. I wasn't sure what to make of her at first.
She was old enough to be my mother, and in a way, as we
became close friends, she became a mother in my new life,
a mentor. We would spend hours in conversation. We went
out together. People wondered, but there was nothing sexual
between us. She was a link between my two lives, a transition out of my past, and she helped me to secure the
emotional roots of my independence.

I moved away five years later and didn't see C again until
I had a phone call from her elder son, who told me she had
cancer. It was 1990, and I hadn't been back for ten years.
I arranged to travel down two days later. The house was

much as I remembered it, but the poverty had gone. There were carpets on all the floors, lamp shades and new curtains and the walls had been repainted. A new three-piece suite surrounded one of those gas fires with fake coal in the grate. C was sitting in an armchair with a blanket over her knees. Her face was drawn and she had lost a lot of weight. There was a faint bluish tinge around the edges of her lips and dark rings around her eyes. She looked very tired.

Her elder son had collected me from the station and then left us to go and shop. I sat on the sofa. C looked at me with some of the old familiarity. She seemed almost like a stranger to me. She told me about her children: her younger son was a labourer; her daughter was married; her elder son was thinking of leaving for London – there was no work in the area. Then she said to me, 'The first time I saw you I knew why you had come here. You were so serious.' I didn't say anything. My seriousness had been frequently remarked on by my mother and I resented it. C told me,

My father was an accountant in Manchester. We were quite a well-off family. But I married beneath myself, as they say. My husband was a seaman. I fell for his charm and his sense of adventure. I longed to escape from home and who better than a sailor to do it with. We made plans to go to Canada. I got a passport. He was going to get me aboard his ship. We would sail into the sunset. I was only nineteen and very romantic, very naive. I thought I would never see my family again, but I didn't care; it seemed worth it.

He got his papers and we travelled down here. It was

27

our first port of call, he said, on the long voyage to a
new life. He could sound romantic too. We married and
a week later he embarked and left me here. I had to keep
at least one part of the dream alive so I never went back
home. I don't think he ever had any intention of taking
me to Canada. I became pregnant and we eventually got
this house. A couple of years later he lost his job and
began to drink. He became violent. I had three kids and
I was at my wits' end. I got an injunction and he left. I
heard he was working the boats. I never saw him again.

I saw C one last time, when she was in hospital. She had
been haemorrhaging and the doctors believed she had only
days to live. She told me about her plans to find a small
flat. She wanted to be on her own and lead her own life. I
nodded my agreement. She repeated that she had always
wanted a place of her own. Her elder son had contacted the
council and thought they might have found somewhere for
her. When I left I held her hand briefly, but she didn't
want to say goodbye, to acknowledge that we might not
see each other again. On the train home I watched the
countryside pass in a swirl of green. We entered a tunnel
and the lights in the train flickered and cut out. For an
instant it was dark and there was nothing to do except
touch the cold, dark glass of the window. And then the
daylight came, and then a hedgerow and, beyond it, fields.
There is never a new beginning, only the muddle of the
past and the never quite graspable present. C died a month
later. She was found by her daughter. She had collapsed in
the kitchen of her new flat, and died alone.

I understood what C had meant about my arrival at her home all those years ago. Like her I had wanted to disown my past. My seriousness had reflected an anxiety that my need for my family would threaten my autonomy. My face would become fixed in earnest concentration as I sought to banish the threatening feelings of dependency. In boyhood, being alone had been something to fear; in adulthood it became a virtue. I bolstered my defences with absolutes, intolerance of compromises and ambiguities. As I grew older I had imagined that at some time in my future, when my own desire was no longer compromised by my need for my mother and my family, I would become myself, and be completely present in my own mind and desire. The illusion of male adolescence is that we can become our idealized fathers, escape our mothers and our need. I now know this is impossible. To imagine that one has escaped from dependency on others is illusory. It is to become enclosed in a self-made emptiness. What was Kerouac's pearl in the end but the terror of his own aloneness, which he could never alleviate because he dreaded his own need of women? His answer was to keep moving. At the end of the road there was nowhere for him to go but back to his childhood home, and no one to be with but his mother. All that journeying, and he ended up where he had begun.

This morning I was alone in my house and I decided to go out for a walk. As I stepped out of the front door the rain began and stopped me. I retreated inside my doorway. The rain became heavier, large drops darkening the dried pavement, gliding down the dusty windows. It began to drum on the ground, pummelling the fragile plants in the window boxes. The woman and her two children from across the road hurried in through their front door. The shopping she carried caught between the children and for a moment they were brought to a halt until she yanked the bags free. The door closed. A car passed. In this unexpected instant activity came to a standstill, and people were cocooned inside their own lives. A second car passed, but more slowly, its tyres swooshing in the water. The rain began to slant into the doorway. For a little while longer I stood watching it. Then I turned back into my house and closed the door. It was a moment in time when there was nowhere to go and nothing to do.

2

MOTHER

The stretched-out hands are alight
in the darkness like an old town.

ZBIGNIEW HERBERT

I

When I walked into the darkened room in the Tate
Gallery in London, three video images were being
projected across one wall. In the left-hand frame a woman is
giving birth. She is crouching, leaning back into somebody's
arms, her muscles straining and contorting with each con-
traction. In the right-hand frame a video camera had
recorded the face of an older woman. She is dying. She lies
perfectly still and silent, her mouth dragged downward by
a stroke, her cheek bones and her skull pressing through
her papery skin, her breath a whisper. Birth and death. And
between the two is the figure of a man floundering under
water, and the sound of a muffled echoing.

Video artist Bill Viola's *Nantes Triptych* is a technological
version of a medieval altarpiece. It runs for approximately
fifteen minutes: the woman struggles to give birth, the man

31

rises and sinks, turning aimlessly in the water, and the older woman lies quite still: the giving, the having and the losing. In life it is women who give and lose. Men want from them. They want the pulse of life first from their mothers, and later in adulthood from the women they love. The man, his features indistinguishable through the blur of the water and the flare of air bubbles which rise to the surface with each immersion, flails blindly between the two: between birth and death, between mother and lover. In the final minutes of the video the woman − Viola's wife − gives birth. The baby emerges from between her legs, and into the arms of the midwife. In the same instant a flicker of life crosses the impassive face of the older woman − Viola's mother − and she dies. Men use art to return to this moment, constantly attempting to understand their journey between these two states, between these two women.

The original story of men's love − in his youth a man escapes from his mother; monogamy brings him back to her. She is always present in the mind's eye of her son, yet she is also always lost. A man remembers the body of his mother; her feel, smell, touch. It gave him life, but its familiarity is also frightening. It reminds him of his childish dependency on her and impels him to try to escape his need of her. The paradox at the heart of men's heterosexuality: desire and need, escape and no escape. Heterosexual love eventually leads back to a man's childhood home, to the loss of his mother as the original object of his love.

The day following my mother's death I went into her bedroom. There were pictures of her mother and father laid beneath a glass top on her bedside table. Cluttered across its surface was a portable radio, a bottle of hand cream, an alarm clock face down, the empty foil of two Disprin tablets and a couple of books. One lay open at the last page she had been reading. There were photographs of our family around the room: my sisters together; my brother; my sister and her new baby; me; me and my son. I switched on the radio to hear what station she had listened to. It was the local radio station and the tinny, slightly earnest sound of the news. Her clothes – jeans and a dark blue sweater – lay folded on the chair as she had left them. The thread that had held all these various objects together, the life which had given meaning to their side-by-sidedness, had gone. The slippers on the floor no longer had any connection to the book on the table. The family photographs, with their insinuations of unity, were broken apart into their different lives. Each item in her wardrobe had its own special memory: a wedding, a party for this dress, a holiday for that. The telephone filled the house with an incessant ringing. Each caller was no longer held to the next by a living presence, but only by a memory which belonged separately to each. Something was finished. She was dead and all that she had held together was now apart.

There was a bloodstain on the carpet, evidence of the paramedics' attempt to revive her. I bent down to touch it. It was still damp from someone's vain effort to wipe it away. Her bed had been stripped, the sheet bundled and the blanket folded. I lifted one of the sheets. It was stained with blood and urine. This sheet seemed to be emblematic of our relationship, its function as a source of childhood comfort subverted by these abject signs of her body. The

33

dearest and the most difficult contained in one place. This is the paradox of my love for my mother: the longing for her to love me in the way I wanted her to, and the desire to be free of my dependency on her.

I kept the sheet my mother had died on for several years, in a plastic carrier bag at the back of one of my drawers. I imagined it, infused with the smell of her, spread out on the floor. As a child I had revolved around my mother's body like a moon, held to her by my need. But I sensed she was always just beyond me, an absence I could find no words to fill. I could never name this void between us; nor could I leave her for long enough to live for myself. Now, after her death, maybe I could put to one side the distance I had established in adulthood, and circle this empty and crestfallen place, and discover the connection between us.

I was unsure what to do with the sheet. I could destroy it. I could burn it or throw it in the dustbin or consign it to a skip (there were always skips around where I lived). In doing so I could release myself from the entrapment of my childhood. I wanted both to keep it and to be rid of it. And so it remained in its plastic bag in my drawer, until one day I stopped my circumambulations and stepped, so to speak, in the middle of the sheet and, remaining there, I finally decided to take it out and burn it. I cleared a space in the back yard and draped it across a large stick. I had no matches, so I lit a piece of screwed-up newspaper from the gas stove and placed it beneath the sheet. The synthetic material mixed with the cotton erupted. The yard is very small and for a moment the heat in the confined space was intense. I was reminded of a Guy Fawkes night when my son was small. I had lit a number of cheap Roman candles and fountains. I had imagined they would be innocuous, but their magnesium brightness and roaring smoke over-whelmed the narrow space between the wall and the side of the house, and I brought them to a premature end with a bucket of water. The flames of my mother's sheet roared. I watched it burn, and felt on my face the fierce energy of the fire. Oily plastic residue dripped onto the concrete.

When I was a child, separation from my mother brought on pangs of inexplicable fear for her safety. I recall one autumn evening when I was ten, looking out of a window at my boarding school, watching the rain fall. I had heard a flood warning on the news and now, as I pressed my face against the glass and watched the headlights of the cars glisten through the rain on the main road beyond the school's walls, I imagined my mother drowning, swept away in a flood tide, her hair spread out and floating like seaweed on the surface of the water. In earlier years, as I lay in bed in the evening, I would call for her to say 'good night' to me. She would arrive in my room, sit on my bedside and kiss me and I would ask her to open my cupboard to make sure there was no demons hiding inside. As soon as she had thrown open the doors to reveal nothing more sinister than my father's old suits and dinner jacket and a few toys, and she had pronounced the words 'goodnight', I was comforted. I took an image of her with me to sleep.

When I grew past this childish phase, I lost the reassur-ance of her presence, and the image of her would sometimes fade as I hovered over sleep and felt myself slipping into another world. At this moment on the cusp of sleep, when sleepers let go of their waking self, I experienced a terror that I would never find myself again. As I sank into sleep I would encounter an emptiness, its nameless, globular form rising up in concentric waves to smother my breathing. I felt myself suffocating and would spring into wakefulness, gasping for air, my eyes snapping open in the dark and my heart thudding. I tried to put off this moment and would stay awake, filling my mind with pleasurable thoughts, sometimes into the early hours of the morning. I would try and slip past its sentinels, and sleep without warning, unknown to myself. I never said any of this to my mother. I don't know why.

At the end of each holiday, before I was due to return to boarding school, she would take me on an outing. The two of us would go out for the day to watch a film, or to eat at a restaurant. One end of summer I had a project on wild flowers to complete. We walked through the woods at the back of our house to a field. We called it the wild flower field. It lay through a railway bridge where, as children, we would yell beneath the Victorian arch and wait for the sound to rebound. It smelt dank and was always muddy. And out on the other side was the wild flower field, a long strip of meadow, bordered by the railway below and woodland above. That summer afternoon my mother and I sat in the field making a perfunctory search for wild flowers. I think we both felt the imminence of my departure for school. My fingers scrabbled through the coarse grass, coming upon a cowslip, or the flower of a wild strawberry, which I picked and placed between sheets of blotting paper, and I would glance across at my mother, on her knees searching, and she would look at me and smile, and in that moment there would be nothing between us but my own sense of emptiness.

We repeated this *tableau vivant*: an evening performance of the film *Tobruk*. We sat together, hearing guns blasting, heroic figures shouting, and then the lull of the desert after the battle. And in this momentary quiet and dark of the cinema I felt numbed. And my mother? She would have loathed the film. A day out to see Steve McQueen in *Grand Prix*. We sat on a seat in a small square, somewhere in central London, my mother voicing her exasperation, the meal ruined by my feeling unwell, the anticipation of the film squandered. Such brief moments laid our relationship bare: the time and the energy which went into maintaining propriety, and the evasions of a nameless dread which neither of us could cope with. And as everything began to unravel, I would abandon myself in compliance with her need to shore up my unhappiness behind the frontispiece of normality. I became my own worst enemy. I remember that film. I lost myself in the speed and excitement. But nothing we did together ever changed the silent fatalism that bound us together.

My mother's childhood in South London had been interrupted by the war. She had been sent to a boarding school and then had moved to the countryside with her parents. Her father was a small businessman whose tastes were continental. He dressed with a fastidious élan which belied his English conservatism. She shared his ambiguous loyalties. A part of her held to the Puritanism of a petit bourgeois culture and the order it gave her. But she disliked its meanness and the sanctimonious hypocrisy it cultivated in the better off. She chose convention. It stifled her, confirmed her desire to escape into something of her own making. But she held to it. The Puritan inside her anchored her against drifting ambivalence. I think she believed that pursuing what she wanted was wrong. She feared it would lead to madness, and to the loss of her sense of belonging. Her own mother had suffered years of mental instability. Addicted to barbiturates, she would phone her psychiatrist at moments of crisis. When she lay dying, she had asked my mother if she loved her and my mother told me she had lied and said that yes she did. Hers had been a solitary childhood which she had palliated with her sense of fun; always the gay, vivacious one in the photographed group of young women. Popular and beautiful, she enjoyed parties and making friends. She had grown adept at hiding her feelings of despair. She expected the same of me when I was sent away to boarding school. I sensed a desperation in her when this did not happen, which left me stunned and pensive. She chivvied me, distracting herself.

My childhood was similar to those of tens of thousands of middle-class English boys growing up in the suburbs in the 1960s. We were the children of men and women who had married in the 1950s. Our families were divided between the domestic world of mothers and the masculine public world of work. Despite the trappings of modern culture, relations between men and women were fashioned on the example of the mid Victorian middle-class family, with its almost feudal ascription of roles. Nature still appeared to determine one's destiny. My mother was the central figure at home; the housekeeper who managed relationships, organized our schooling, bought clothes, birthday cards, food; arranged holidays; cooked and entertained. Her work produced the family – myself, my two sisters, my brother. My father, on the other hand, was a more peripheral figure in family life. He left home each morning at 7.05 for the City of London and returned at 7 p.m. Every Saturday morning he took us to the sweet shop, then went to the pub. In the afternoon he worked in the garden. On Sunday he returned to the garden and in the evening went to the pub again. Our family life was maternal. The language of emotions – of need, pleasure and pain – were profoundly feminized.

The years after the war had witnessed the promotion of this kind of family. A growing number of childcare experts reinforced this division of roles by emphasizing women's natural inclination to be mothers and their instinctive need for a child. In a series of radio broadcasts in 1944 D. W. Winnicott had introduced the public to the idea that the psychological health of children was determined by the quality of mothering they received. John Bowlby postulated his theory of human attachment, originating the term 'maternal deprivation' to describe the consequence to children of an inadequate bond with their mother. In 1958 Benjamin Spock published *Baby and Child Care* and gradually supplanted Truby King's orthodoxy with his more intuitive approach to mothering. A new emphasis was placed on a woman's empathy with her child. Mothers and children were fixed and frozen into domesticity, in service to the child's developmental needs. This promotion of women as mothers provoked a misogynistic backlash. Motherhood came under renewed scrutiny from welfare agencies, academics and social commentators. Following research in the United States it was claimed that mothers were overprotecting their children and failing to allow them to separate. A woman's domestic power and her control in the middle-class home was seen as a potential threat to male dominance. Jimmy Porter in John Osborne's 1956 play *Look Back in Anger* railed against the influence of women: 'No, there is nothing for it, me boy, but to let yourself be butchered by the women.' The drama of this historically specific family – the domestic division of labour, the polarization of masculinity and femininity, the misogyny and the male anxieties and fantasies about the power and influence of mothers – introduced the spectre of the doting, overprotective mother, who smothered her children and undermined their capacity to become independent adults.

The mother–son relationship was subject to particular attention, and this is still the case in all classes and among all ethnic groups. To different degrees, a boy's need for his mother is seen as shameful and effeminate. Social attitudes cultivate in boys a pseudo independence, in which a boy's need for his mother is repressed and denied. He is forced to relinquish his attachment to his mother prematurely. The mother is lost as an object of love. Freud writes of this loss in his essay 'Mourning and Melancholia': 'one feels a loss . . . has occurred, but one cannot see clearly what it is that has been lost.' Grief at this loss holds the boy prisoner to his mother. Unable to mourn, his capacity to love another is inhibited. The mother assumes an omnipotence in the unconscious of her son, because only she can satisfy his need.

40

She becomes a threatening figure at the gateway to male freedom and desire, the original gorgon who will deny her son his potency and transform him into a block of stone. Adrienne Rich has described this male fantasy of the mother: she is 'controlling, erotic, castrating, heart suffering, guilt-ridden and guilt-proving; between her legs snakes; on her lap a helpless infant or a martyred son'.

As he grows up, a boy idealizes his mother at the same time as he hates her, an ambivalence he later brings to his relationships with other women. When I began to try to understand how this relationship had shaped my life I turned to Freud. His ideas pervade our common-sense understanding of how masculinity is formed in our childhood struggle to become independent from our parents. For Freud the father was the central, most important figure of family life. In his 1909 essay 'Family Romances' he argued that a boy's rivalry with his father in the Oedipus complex meant that he battled to be free of his father rather than his mother. But as I was growing up in 1960s Britain, the problems of my independence centred around my mother. Freud was not so helpful in understanding this issue of separation and the role of motherhood in the making of masculinity. Much of his comments on the subject reproduced his own society's idealization and demonization of mothers. While he praised the special bond between mother and son in several of his essays, his glowing remarks do not disguise the 'terrifying impression of helplessness' he felt in a boy's dependence on his mother. He argued that a mother naturally projected her thwarted ambitions onto men: 'even marriage is not made secure until the wife has succeeded in making her husband her child as well as acting as mother to him.' It has been the mother, not the father, who has been the psychologically dominant figure in the family. I struggled to be free of my mother, and at the same time I did not want to be parted from her.

II

I was fourteen and walking with my mother up the high street, five paces behind, ashamed of being with her, but reluctant to lose sight of her in the crowd. We'd been shopping for clothes – clothes she wanted for me. On the other side of the high street there was a large gang of skinheads. Boys my age and older cut a swathe through the shoppers; their bald heads and Doc Martens and tight jeans and sharp-cut Ben Shermans condensed their bodies into hard, clear, dispassionate lines. I imagined them glancing across at me, and felt the humiliation of trailing behind my mother. I wanted my feet encased in a pair of strong, masculine, industrial boots. I had saved my money and several weeks later I bought a pair, ankle high, but not too thick soled. My mother disapproved. We fought over clothes as we'd later argue around politics: bell bottoms, loons, three-button shirts with Indian embroidery, army surplus great coats, patched jeans and patched denim jackets and long, badly cut hair, later to be displaced by the regalia of punk rock – black drainpipes, motifed shirts, pierced ears and dyed hair. Clothes were a battle between our competing ideas of who and what I was to be.

I conjured up my future when I left school. It was a world far removed from my mother. I would live on a croft, a commune, a kibbutzim. I'd take off and hitch-hike anywhere. I bought copies of *OZ* and *International Times* and fashioned images of my future life. I projected myself into the world with abandon, and in my dreaming, in the corner of the frame, was the woman I would find and fall in love with. When I met her, I could finally become myself. After I had left school, a few weeks before my eighteenth birthday, I caught a train with a friend, M, to what was then Yugoslavia. I had no plans. We sat for two days and nights cocooned in our compartment, an assortment of travellers passing through as the train crossed Europe. When we reached our destination I found myself unceremoniously pitched out into a strange world. Here was my freedom. I had money and my possessions in my backpack. We hitch-hiked to the coast. Young people hung around the squares of the small towns, sleeping rough. Here were my halcyon days, but I stalled at their prospect. I had brought with me all the ambivalence of my childhood. I felt intimidated by these worldly, confident young people. I felt I'd removed myself from my own life to a place in which I couldn't live. I wanted to return home, and yet I didn't want to be at home with my family, with my mother: I was here to get away from her. I carried this dilemma with me for several weeks as we hitch-hiked up towards Germany. One night we camped in a small pine forest on a hillside in the Piedmont. It was Sunday morning and I awoke early to the sounds of the bells from the church across the valley. Our tent was very small and M was still sleeping, so I disentangled myself from my sleeping bag and crawled out. The dead and brown pine needles which carpeted the ground were damp and chilly from the dew. There was a mist in the valley, and the church, built on a rising slope, was just visible. I wondered where I was. I knew the geography of my position, but I had no sense of my self in the world. I felt strangely bereft.

My hitch-hike through Europe was a salutary experience. I recall that Sunday as a frustrating attempt to reach Munich. It took us two days, and on our arrival I became ill and was admitted to hospital with acute appendicitis. I spent a week in hospital, and then I returned home, my bid for independence brought to a premature, but not unwelcome, end. I enrolled in a sixth-form college to study for my A-levels and the following year, when I was nineteen, I went to university. It was a safer, if more pedestrian way of leaving home. I fell in love with a woman on campus. I watched her ride her bike and I plotted ways I could accidentally cross her path. I noticed she went to a folk club so I joined and stood beside her, intoxicated by her closeness. After several weeks I invented an excuse to speak to her. She was slight and German and wore her hair in a crew cut. She told me she was a Maoist and she talked in a soft, slightly clipped accent. She was twenty-four. She lived with two other medical students in a smart house not far from the university and I began to visit her regularly. She soon grew tired of my attentions and I, failing to discover the magic suggested by her appearance, became disenchanted. My passion slowly evaporated. The image of her, which had once seemed to personify my future,

44

disappeared. I left university that summer and she returned to Germany.

One day that August I was cycling down a road close by to where I was working. It was hot, and there were few cars on the road. I noticed a woman walking on the far side of the road who reminded me of that German student. She attracted me in the same way. She was with a man and they were talking together. I stopped my bike and watched them pass. I did not see her again but the image of her remained with me. Two years passed and one morning, at breakfast, this woman walked into the kitchen of the house I was living in. She was on holiday and staying with a man called P who had recently moved in. She introduced herself as F. She became a frequent visitor. We became friends and then lovers. She invited me to stay with her. This was before I had moved to London, before we had ideas of living together. I caught the train north, to her home town. She lived in a street of red-brick back-to-backs, close to the old docks. It was the weekend and on the Sunday we walked along the canal. I felt a curious sense of detachment and, sensing this, she asked me what was wrong. I told her that since the train had drawn into the station and I'd seen her waiting for me on the platform, I'd experienced an involuntary distancing of myself from her. An obstacle had come between us. That evening we watched a film on the television about two young women hitch-hiking around Switzerland. I was reminded of my own rather dismal experience, and of that damp hillside in Austria. Being with F, I felt as I had done then. Something had closed off inside me.

During our first years together I experienced this feeling

several times. On one occasion, when F was pregnant, I sat in the launderette looking at her while she was reading and I felt as if I was standing in front of a wall, looking for some niche or opening, and could find only dark granite. And I was on the inside of this wall. This lasted several days. When I was able to talk to her about it, my feelings for her returned. I've become aware of the uncanny quality of heterosexual love. Sexual desire, which impels us into the future in search of lovers, returns us to our need for our mothers. This need was the wall of non-feeling I experienced. At the heart of men's relationships with women are desire and need. Desire is associated with the father, with language and culture. It is active, searching and assertive. It leads us into the future, and as men grow up it becomes an essential part of their masculinity. Need, on the other hand, is associated with our mothers and is seen as instinctual, passive and wordless. We imagine it belongs to the past, to our childhood. Men's heterosexuality is a conflict between sexual desire and emotional dependency, the latter continually threatening to diminish the former. This embattled quality to men's sexuality finds its expression in culture as men endeavour to resolve their inner conflict by keeping the objects of their desire separate from the objects of their need.

J. M. Barrie's *Peter Pan* is the perennial story of men's need – the mother's boy who cannot grow up. It is an adventure story with a difference. Instead of journeying overseas, Barrie turned inwards, into his own unconscious, to create Neverland, a symbolic metaphor for the male psyche. 'Desperate attempt to grow up but can't,' he commented in his diary. In his novel *Tommy and Grizel* (1900) Barrie anticipated the themes of Peter Pan: 'He was a boy only ... And boys cannot love. Oh is it not cruel to ask a boy to love? ... He was a boy who could not grow up.' When Peter Pan is confronted with the desires of Wendy, Tinkerbell and Tiger-Lily, he denies sexual desire and misunderstands their demands as their maternal longing to meet his own childish insecurity.

> PETER. Now what is it you want?
> TIGER-LILY. Want to be your Squaw.
> PETER. Is that what you want, Wendy?
> WENDY. I suppose it is, Peter.
> PETER. Is that what you want, Tink?
> *Bells answer.*
> PETER. You all three want that. Very well – that's really wishing to be my mother.

Peter Pan is an allegory of the sexual and emotional predicament of middle-class men. Neither child nor adult, Peter Pan is narcissistic and asexual. He longs for a mother, yet is unable to endure any form of emotional dependency. Misogyny and childish emotions alternate in his attempts to free himself from his need. He fantasizes about his omnipotence, takes risks with his life and boasts in an attempt to rid himself of the mournful child he really is. Time future for English manliness, like the infamous clock whose silence would signal Hook's death, stops around adolescence.

The allegory of *Peter Pan* remains relevant to men's contemporary relationships with women. The middle-class family in the second half of the century has reproduced a masculinity which similarly perpetuated adolescence into adulthood. One of the most eloquent observers of this predicament has been the German film-maker Wim Wenders. In his 1985 film *Paris, Texas* Wenders gives an account of the emotional lives of men who came of age in the 1960s. Film critic Kraft Wetzel has likened Wenders to a small boy who refuses to grow up; a man who prefers the romantic nostalgia of childhood to adult relationships. And there is truth in this: *Paris, Texas* is a contemporary version of *Peter Pan*.

The central character, Travis, is taken ill in the Texas desert and his brother Walt travels down from Los Angeles to bring him home. When he arrives Travis refuses to speak. Walt is frustrated by Travis's enigmatic silence. Where has he been for the last four years? He tells Travis that he and his wife Ann are looking after Travis's young son Hunter. Travis's wife Jane has also vanished; they haven't seen her since she left the boy on their doorstep four years previously. When Travis finally speaks, he asks Walt, 'Did you ever go to Paris?' He shows him a small battered photograph of a vacant lot he has bought in Paris, a tiny hamlet in the Texas desert. He had been searching for this place because, he informs Walt, this is where he was conceived: 'I figured that's where I began . . . Travis Clay Henderson. I started out there.'

When they arrive in Los Angeles, Travis tells his son he is going to search for the boy's mother, who is living in Houston. Hunter asks if he can accompany him, and they set off together. They find Jane and follow her to a peep joint where she works. Travis enters one of the booths,

48

and through the one-way mirror he watches her come into the room. He picks up the telephone and begins to tell her a story about a man who was so deeply in love with his young wife that he couldn't bear to be apart from her. He gave up his work so that they could be together. They were very happy. But when their son was born he began to feel excluded and jealous. He imagined that she was going out meeting other men, and so he began locking her in the trailer where they lived. He tied her up at night to stop her from running away. Eventually she managed to escape. When the man awoke his wife and child had disappeared and he panicked and ran and didn't stop running.

Travis distrusts love because he has inherited the sins of his father. Before he meets Jane, he tells Hunter:

> 'My mother was not a fancy woman . . . she never pretended to be a fancy woman.'
> 'Then what was she?'
> 'She was just plain, good, just very good. My daddy had this idea in his head, a kind of sickness, this idea about her. He looked at her but didn't see her. He saw this idea. He told people she was from Paris. It was a big joke . . . he started believing it. Oh God! She'd get so embarrassed.'

For Travis, a man's sexual love for women is a 'kind of sickness'. His journey to Houston to find Jane is not as a husband seeking reconciliation with his wife. It is to find a mother for his son, and also for himself – for the boy he was and still is. The reunion of Hunter and his mother –

the final scene – is the only moment of love and intimacy in the film. They hold each other and whirl around the hotel room. Outside, Travis looks up at the hotel building and then climbs into his truck and drives away. Wenders offers no way out of this bleak masculine world of loss and estrangement. Desire for women recalls men's longing for maternal love, which inhibits or corrupts sexual love. *Paris, Texas* implies that men cannot reconcile this dilemma. Travis is fated to a liminal existence without a home or the prospect of love.

Freud has summed up this predicament of male heterosexuality: where men 'love they do not desire and where they desire they do not love. They seek objects they do not need to love in order to keep their sensuality away from the objects they love.' Men are wary of women. They conjure a language likening 'woman' to nature, the flesh subordinate to men's reason: Mother Earth, green fields, lush pastures that men can bask in, that feed us. But this fantasy of 'woman' also encompasses the mud and the dirt of women's bodies that invokes disgust – the menstrual blood, the female sexual desire that instils anxiety in men. She is the landscape we contemplate with admiration and ever after instils in us the anxiety that she will swallow us up. She is the maternal body from which we must separate ourselves. And she is the temptress, the harlot who threatens our self-control. The mother and the whore, two archetypes of femininity invented by men to distance our need for a mother's love from our sexual desire. Men debase women to safeguard their sexual desire.

Culture has divided men and women into victim sons

and abject mothers. Horror films such as Rob Reiner's *Misery* explore the uncanny ability of the maternal body to disturb and instil fear. Following a car accident in a snow storm, the writer Paul Sheldon is rescued by Annie Wilkes, a former nurse, who takes him to her remote house. Here he is precipitated back into a state of infancy. He recovers consciousness to discover that he has two broken legs and is entirely dependent on her care. It transpires that Annie Wilkes has been spying on him and was tailing him before he crashed. She is, she exclaims ecstatically, his Number One Fan, and she is obsessed with the life of Misery, the heroine of Sheldon's popular romances. Disturbed by her increasingly irrational behaviour, Sheldon discovers that her nursing career was brought to an end after the inexplicable deaths of children in her care. Trapped and fearful for his life, Sheldon is forced to make a desperate and violent attempt to escape 'Mother' and he bludgeons Annie Wilkes to death.

Men defend themselves by turning their need for women into contempt. In the early years of this century the writer Henry James associated the rise of popular culture with femininity when he wrote: 'the masculine tone is passing out of the world. It is a feminine, nervous, hysterical, chattering, canting age.' Men try to talk their way out of their difficult and threatening sense of dependency. Violence is the consequence when men fail to find the words they need. When women speak, men are confronted with their impotence. My sister and I fought and argued as children. Her weapons were words; mine were whatever came to hand. To shield myself from her disparaging and piercing remarks, I resorted to physical violence. A fist, kick, shove versus her cutting, wounding remarks – 'it's true, it's true, you are!' Unable to answer back, I hit out. What now do we do as adult men? We keep our distance and fashion a masculine tone of language designed to exclude women. If we are trapped and beaten with words, we can become enraged. Some men attack, taunt, humiliate their wives and partners because they are gripped with a hatred born of their dependency. A violent man does not leave his wife. He is terrified of being alone, yet he cannot bear to live with her because she is a constant reminder of his own childish insecurity. He uses violence in an attempt to master her in order to master his own inner turmoil. He instils terror in order to maintain the fragile equilibrium of his emotional life. Dust on the mantelpiece, an ornament out of place, the baby crying, a young daughter wanting pocket money, the wife who has spent an extra ten pounds, a meal not to his liking – disorder, chaos, dissolution. When he has vented his rage, he will weep and beg forgiveness like a small boy who has run away from his mother and found her again.

There is no more graphic illustration of men's fear and hatred of this emotional need than the story of Michael Ryan, who shot dead fourteen people in Hungerford in 1987. After his rampage through the town he was cornered in one of the classrooms in his old school. He repeatedly asked about his mother: 'Is she all right?' He apologized if he had hurt her and told the policemen that he didn't mean her any harm. She was his first victim; the second was a woman he came across having a picnic with her two children. He tried to rape her and failed. From then on 'the enemy' was everywhere. Newspaper reports of the murders were full of small-town gossip about Ryan's relationship with his mother and his inability to be independent of her. The byline of the *Daily Express* read: DOTING MOTHER'S LAVISH GIFTS TURNED RYAN INTO A SPOILT WIMP. A neighbour, Mr Brian Meikle, said: 'He was a real mother's boy . . . he was no Rambo, he was quiet and shy, more like a Bambi.' Another described him as 'a real mother's boy, a spoilt little wimp'. Mrs Rowland commented: 'I remember him as a spoilt person and the only person I ever remember seeing with him was his mother, who adopted a very protective attitude concerning her son . . . he was moody, sulky. But he was not the type of boy who got involved in fighting. He was an introvert and a bit of a mystery.' She added, 'I never saw him with a girlfriend.' The press commentary described Ryan as a failure, citing his inadequacy and inability to live up to the cultural and sexual expectations of other men. Ryan had struggled to assert his manliness. He had been obsessed with guns. According to friends he had boasted and fantasized about being a crack army paratrooper. Humiliated and trapped in his dependency, perceiving his mother as a persecutor whom he could neither leave nor live with, Ryan exploded.

Mothers have been incidental to the stories of masculinity, but they are ubiquitous. It is as if they are the unwritten beginning from which men are always departing. And the end? The end is also in the beginning. In the beginning is touch and feel and smell, not the word. There is no distance between a mother and her infant. She is omnipresent and indivisible. And then a space opens. Her absence is the original loss which instils in us that determination to know and to understand ourselves. Language is the reward for giving up this intimacy. And yet that essential loss exists just beyond our comprehension. Writing about my mother is an attempt to find words to understand my relationship with her. And it is also a ritual of separation from her, a clumsy breaking away and assertion of individuality. It is a gesture of intent which dissembles itself. In the words I put on paper I search for my identity. In writing I am looking for her again.

I want to return now to the sheet that I burnt, because I wonder what it was that induced me to destroy it. The night after my mother died I had a dream about her. I dreamed that I was at a festival, sitting in a field with F and our son. A woman began to sing. She had a strong, powerful voice. She sang about 'the man she was looking for' and made it obvious that she had feelings for me. When she had completed her song she climbed into a London taxi. I climbed in after her and sat opposite on one of those pull-down seats. She said to me: 'You made the song, you can send and you can give, but the question is, can you fool?' I said that wasn't such an easy thing and waited a while. But I wanted nothing from her and said goodbye to her and shook her hand. I told her how fine her voice was, and then I went back to my family.

It appears to be a dream about loss and reconciliation, but there is something in it which remains ambiguous. What did she mean by 'can you fool?' An answer lay in the sheet I had kept. As a child I wanted to discover the nature of the emptiness I felt between my mother and me. When

54

I spread the sheet on the floor, it becomes an empty space in which I can wait until my mother's face appears. A wild fleeting glimmer of panic crosses her face because in this space lies the despair which was her greatest fear. She attempts to repress her feelings with a smile and I experience a familiar desire to escape, and then, in the same instant, the need to stay with her. I simply wait until I have swallowed both these conflicting feelings. Like an amoeba I envelop her pain until I feel the cell of my body digesting it. As a young child I had experienced my separation from her as a form of death. In retrospect my fear was not that I would die in her absence, but that she would die in mine. Then I too would be unable to live. It was necessary to remain with her always in order to keep her alive. But as a child I could never catch up with her for long enough to make her stop to hold me and to love me, so that when I grew up I could leave her for long enough to live and bid her goodbye. I wanted to get to the bottom of the mess that was between us, to find out what was really there and to end all my chasing. Leave or stay, stay or leave, I had oscillated between the two, never able to be still. But here on this sheet, the two of us sit together in a circle of white and nothing distracts us. Perhaps now, the words I needed to fill the absence between us can take root.

Can I fool her? I understood what she meant. To fool with another woman is an invitation to commit adultery. No, in the early years of my relationship with F I could never entirely let go of my mother. It was like a shutter closing down inside me. I now understand what Kerouac meant when he wrote, 'somewhere along the line the pearl would be handed me'. Kerouac's pearl is the reconciliation of need and desire. It is the capacity of a man to both love his mother and be able to live for himself.

3

FATHER

'father when he passed on, left dust'

A. K. RAMANUJAN

I

When I was a boy we would spend August on the Isle of Wight in a house by the sea. One particular year – I was no more than seven – my father and I would go on a daily walk together. One afternoon – it was to be our last walk of the holiday – we were following a path through a small copse and I held his hand as he pointed out to me various species of birds and plants. And I, taking pleasure in this intimacy, had asked him, as we approached the house we were staying in, how far we had walked. He told me we had walked ten miles. When we arrived back I rushed to tell my mother that we had walked ten miles. It seemed an extraordinary achievement. It was not so much the distance, but the fact that my father and I had accomplished this feat together. In adulthood, looking back, I don't believe that we walked such a distance. My father had

57

knowingly, and with the best of intentions, exaggerated. But that is beside the point. That day he cast his light on me.

I remember when I was about eleven years old, I visited him at his office. I caught the train into town with my mother. It was a small room with a number of large desks, each with several telephones. He was using one of these when we were shown into the room. He spoke with the assured and confident voice of a man who knew his business. He adopted a similar manner with me when he showed me round, introducing me to the other men he worked with, who were polite to my mother and gracious to me. He was a man who was doing well and I was his son. But it was a strange, intimidating world in which both my mother and I were out of place. He was happy and demonstrative, and I wondered if this was the same man who was my father, because at home he was much more reticent. He would often stand on his own in the living room, a drink in his hand, looking out of the window. This is how he was when he came home from work, standing or sitting, saying very little. I wanted to know what he was thinking about, or whether he simply banished all thoughts from his mind and just stared into nothing, exhausted by his day's work.

As I grew older my father and I had little in common to talk about. A distance opened up between us which was occasionally bridged by an outing to a rugby match, a game for which we shared an enthusiasm. During the South African Springbok's tour of 1970, my father bought tickets for the climactic game against the Lions at Twickenham. The touring team were training at my father's old rugby club.

I was excited by a photograph in the *Daily Telegraph* of a club official indignantly tearing up an anti-apartheid poster that he had snatched from the hands of a demonstrator. I cut it out in approval of his actions. There had been large and often violent demonstrations against the tour, and when we arrived at Twickenham there were phalanxes of police surrounding the massed crowds of demonstrators. I walked beside my father eyeing this alien and threatening gathering with a nervous disdain. During the game we sat in the stand, eating chicken drumsticks prepared by my mother. We were surrounded by the hip flasks and camel coats of the home counties. This masculine crowd cheered with a vindictive glee whenever a demonstrator was flattened as he ran across the pitch in an attempt to disrupt the game. As I grew older I wanted my father to explain such things to me. He was never a belligerent man in his politics; I gained the impression he was uninterested. I had to find out by myself, and this finding out soon became an act of distancing myself still further from him. The year I refused to stand for the national anthem at Twickenham – I think I was eighteen years old – marked the end of our rugby matches together. He wasn't angry with me, only uncomprehending, and I wanted, more than anything, for him to understand me.

For several years after this he would mention rugby to me as if I still retained my old enthusiasm for it. On returning home from work he would push open the door of my bedroom and stand there, leaning in, and say something for small talk – perhaps a comment about the garden, his day at work, the weather – and, as time went by, I would barely acknowledge him. After a while he stayed away. I was relieved, but also at a loss. I hated him for not knowing what I wanted him to know about me.

His reticence at home while I was growing up meant that I remembered his comments about the weather. It was a means of beginning a conversation, even if it did stall after a few sentences. He might remark on the sky or mention the forecast, particularly if he believed it was going to rain. He liked to watch the rain; he would complain he'd be unable to mow the lawn, and the wonder when he would be able to cut it, concerned it would grow untidy. Perhaps he simply wanted to talk about something. In a curious way I took comfort in his meteorological predictions, not because they were always right,, but because I imagined that in some indeterminate way they were his attempt to smooth our way into the future, and guarantee us a safe passage. Perhaps he saw the unpredictable weather as a test which demanded that he calculate a constant path through all life's eventualities. This, it seemed to me, was the nature of fathering; to walk with us into the future. I imagined that somewhere in his silence he had honed such a constancy, a rhythm of time and space uniquely his own. I was always waiting for that moment when he'd reveal this to me, as if somewhere about his person he had hidden what I most wanted. Whenever I was alone with him this tension would be present, and it made it difficult to talk.

When I phoned home from school it was always my mother I wanted to speak to – 'Hello, Dad, is Mum there?' – and he'd pass the phone over to her. It was only after my mother died that I began to talk to my father. I would phone, knowing he would have no one to pass the phone on to and so escape from a difficult, stumbling, hesitant and very brief exchange. Somewhere between us had been my mother, and now we were like two strangers converging from opposite sides of the world looking for common ground. After one of my earlier visits to his house I was driven by my father back to the local train station. As we turned into the approach road, the lights of the level crossing began to flash and the barriers descended. He accelerated, two wheels mounting the pavement to squeeze past the queue of cars, and turned into the station car park just as the train drew to a halt. I jumped out of the car and ran for the bridge to cross the tracks. Before my foot was on the second step the train had pulled out of the station. My father was reversing his car. I lifted my hand to signal him to stop; to say goodbye; perhaps to sit in his car for thirty minutes until the next train. But I hesitated – not wanting the discomfort of the silence between us – and he drove out of the car park without a backward glance.

A man remembers the body of his mother; her feel, smell, touch. For each man, his mother is the object of his passionate desire for life. And yet, paradoxically, she embodies the helplessness of his fate. 'Father' is the illusion of a benign saviour who will guarantee us our future, even our immortality. Men are always looking for a symbolic father – the machinery of organizations, the engines of public life, the mechanics of ambition and money-making and the recognition or adulation of others – which will protect them from their love for their mothers. James Joyce once wrote that 'fatherhood is a legal fiction'. It is a cultural and psychological relationship and for this reason it always feels tenuous and incomplete. A father's transcendent power is sought in the surrogates of the divine rule of providence, or a political doctrine, or a religious faith. In their life stories men search for a father. They pursue an image of him, a wish for his Name, House and Law. In my childhood my father's detachment from the messy, unending emotional business of domestic life – we were never allowed into the bathroom in the mornings while he was 'shaving' – gave him an aura of mystery. His role as head of household was grounded in, and could only survive on the basis of, his not being known. Fathers are like wraiths; unlike mothers, they seem to have no substance to them.

A great many men claim that their fathers never revealed their love to them; their own desire to be recognized and embraced went unacknowledged. Men have been anxious about touching and holding their sons, a fear which borders on the homophobic. What they have denied in themselves – their love for their mothers, their intimacy and sensuality – they have denied to their sons. Men will offer boys a small punch of greeting, or an affectionate ruffling of hair, but they hold back from the unconditional trust of surrendering their bodies. Men cannot easily accept a young boy's sensuality because it is a reminder of everything they have been forced to give up. The paucity of emotional contact between fathers and sons goads men into cynicism towards their fathers or an often fruitless search for their love. We scour the past for moments of intimacy. Their rarity makes them precious – when he smiled at me and kissed me; he held my hand; he listened; he praised; he touched me. The smallest tactile, sensual memory in which a father's body is experienced in the same way as a mother's consoles us. In Duane Michals's photograph *Letter from My Father* a teenage boy stands sideways on to the camera, his face set, preoccupied with some inner thought. Behind him stands his father, hands on his hips, truculent, his mouth fixed in exasperation, looking at the boy. Next to him, partly obscured by the boy, is the mother, a peripheral figure in this drama between father and son. Above the image and below it, Michals has written his letter in a scrawled handwriting.

> As long as I can remember, my father always said to me that one day he would write me a very special letter. But he never told me what the letter would be about. I used to try and guess what I would read in the letter, what mystery, what family secret could at last be revealed. I know what I had hoped to reveal in the letter. I wanted him to tell me where he had hidden his affection. But then he died and the letter never did arrive, and I never found that place where he had hidden his love.

Our attachment to our mothers can overwhelm us. With our fathers we cling to the threads of our contact with them and weave them into something intelligible; we try to give them substance and meaning, because out of them we create our sense of future. A man makes of his father what he can – a distant man, barely known and yet harboured deep inside, both in his presence and in his absence – since he first turned away from his mother's face and recognized that there was more in the world than the two of them.

A boy offers his father countless maps to guide him into

the stray corners of the world where he is unable to venture alone. Encountering only silence, he will grow contemptuous of his father's weakness and of the way in which he hovers on the edge of family life. In adulthood, this adolescent contempt remains, perpetuated by a man's apprehension of his father's disapproval. Franz Kafka, in an attempt to exorcize the strangulating hold his father held him in, wrote 'A Letter to His Father'. 'What was always incomprehensible to me was your total lack of feeling for the suffering and shame you could inflict on me with your words and judgments.' Even in adulthood, men succumb to childhood awkwardness when they crave a father's approval and receive only his silence. Without his acknowledgement they feel shame, resenting him for their humiliation. It's the subject of Paul Durcan's poem 'Mother's Boy':

> You bought a racehorse
> in your barrister days
> And called it after me –
> Mother's Boy.
> It was a chestnut colt
> And I recall dark days
> Of delight in the 1950s
> Bringing water to the red horse.
>
> It won nothing
> And cost you money –
> Like me.
> If you could live your life again
> Which would you choose,
> Your racehorse or me?

Father

Durcan declares for the racehorse; 'you'd choose your racehorse / And so would I'. Men's contempt for a father's failings reflects their own sense of worthlessness. Behind the masquerade of self-assurance is the half-recognized knowledge that fathers and sons share a longing to be encompassed by a mother; whether divided, competing, united or estranged, fathers and sons know the truth of each other. In 'The Two Little Boys at the Back of the Bus' Durcan describes this unacknowledged collusion. Father and son are united in a morbid and inert existence.

Safe in the back of the bus
At seventy-two you share your biscuits with me,
Your packet of digestive biscuits,
As we head back down the Stillorgan Road
To Mother.
Mother will meet us at the bus station
And drive us out to the plane
Which she will pilot herself,
A Fokker 50.
When we are safely ensconced
At an altitude of seventeen thousand feet
Turning left at Liverpool for Preston,
She will come down from the cockpit
And put us both to sleep
With an injection of Sodium Amytal.
Isn't that what we've always yearned for,
Father and Son,
To be old, wise, male savages in our greatness
Put to sleep by Mother?

This is the bequest of patrimony when men's possessions, status symbols and various types of material power are put to one side. Father, an emotional sibling of his own son, his love for him tempered by his desire for and competition over the same woman, can only offer a sham of authority. This is why men and boys hero-worship other men. Heroes are the sons they wish they had been; they are loved and elevated by their fathers.

A father's ideal love is his understanding, which provides us with the self-knowledge to grow out of our mothers and into our own lives. If we can unlock the enigma of our fathers, reach back into our pasts and beyond, into our pre-history – a father's life before we arrived – we imagine we might discover the knowledge of who we are, the understanding of ourselves with which our fathers have been unable to provide us. When fathers die our hope for this understanding can be extinguished, and nothing will lie between us and our own death. John Fowles, in his poem 'Chalkwell Park', describes taking his ailing father on a Sunday stroll. They inspect the flowers, but all the time Fowles has in mind his father's impending death.

> and death
>
> I cannot say
> swift passage
> I cannot say
> most natural thing
> and cannot say
> cannot say

he mumbles on
'I thought it would be fine,
the glass was high'
cannot say
do not die
my father my father do not die.

When Father has died, all that has remained unsaid is piled
like a snow drift over the years, burying in its silence his
fugitive figure. There is an urgency, a need to put words
to this receding figure, to bring him back and find, in his
death, the connection which eluded him in life. Paul Auster,
in *The Invention of Solitude*, describes hearing the news of his
father's death. 'Even before we packed our bags and set out
on the three hour drive to New Jersey, I knew that I would
have to write about my father.' In the early 1990s men were
following the example of Auster. They were writing about
their fathers, in search of themselves.

Nick Hornby's *Fever Pitch*, Blake Morrison's *And When
Did You Last See Your Father?*, Paul Watkins's *Stand Before
Your God* and Richard Rayner's *The Blue Suit* are stories
which have at their centre the death, duplicity or absence
of a father. 'Autobiography', wrote John Berger, 'begins
with a sense of being alone.' The filial language of these
autobiographies – loss, fear, shame, betrayal, disappointment, resentment, misunderstanding – resonates with that
aloneness. Men do not look to women for respite from this
aloneness; rather women are perceived to be the cause of
men's confusions about their roles and masculine identities.
The promise of certitude for these men, their hope of belong-

ing, lies with their fathers. 'Even before his death he had been absent . . .' writes Paul Auster. 'If, while he was alive, I kept looking for him, kept trying to find the father who was not there, now that he is dead I still feel as though I must go on looking for him.' Preoccupied with paternal absence, these autobiographies make symbolic substitutions for the father and express fantastical longings for his presence. They desire to immobilize his transient, slippery always-just-beyond-reach-ness; they puzzle over his enigma and seek to discover the place where he hid his love. Each has written for his father and, in recompense for exposing himself, makes a request: that the father acknowledge that, like his son, he too, despite his constant, strenuous efforts, failed to win the approval of his own father: a mutual humbling, a mutual love, an agreement to redesign the old male agenda on relationships and find a place to begin speaking.

In the stultified, disassociated language of masculinity this searching for identity begins with the death of the father. A literal death, but also a metaphorical expression for the ordinariness and failures of paternal love in the face of grandiose expectations; an indefinable sense of hopelessness. A recognition, as Auster writes, that right from the start 'the essence of this project is failure'. Perhaps in the end there is no secret for sons to discover. For men brought up in the 1940s there was no expressive language of domesticity; feelings were repressed or directed into serving their families, coping and doing their duty. The emotional reticence of this generation of fathers is part of their masculinity, born of a particular social order with a clear and

68

distinct separation between the private and the public, between feminine feeling and masculine restraint. That has changed, and with it what men want from their fathers. But there is no hidden, magical reservoir of love, only their own romanticized patina constructed out of contemporary expectations of intimacy. The private dramas portrayed in these autobiographies of men seeking the approval and love of their fathers are a product of larger social forces, of an epochal way of life, of a form of paternity that is historically ending. The post-sixties generation of men clashed with the old ways of their fathers, and were left without any sense of continuity. This alienation has provoked an intense desire to 'find' their fathers and to regain a sense of belonging. Of all the writers it is Morrison who has the deepest under-standing of this paradox and the wider sense that the private language of autobiography speaks of broader forces of change: 'The days of fathers and sons are over: they've run the heredity business for themselves, have invested all their names and money in it, and now the fathers are dying and the sons not taking over and the whole shebang's in ruins.'

II

On my chest of drawers I have a snapshot of my son and myself, taken in a photo booth. I think he is about three years old. It was a habit then, when we went out together, to photograph ourselves in a booth. I have a small collection of these passport photos in my wallet, but this particular one has remained foremost. He is standing on my lap with his arm around my neck. I am absorbed in the business of having my photograph taken, and he has pressed his cheek to the side of my head, and glances at the camera out of the corner of his eyes. It is not he who is displayed for the camera, so much as his love for me. When I look at this picture, taken almost fourteen years ago, I see his absolute trust. It is a reminder to be grateful for the pure pleasure I found in his love, but also to consider the nature of a father's love.

To me, my son's birth was wonderful, a little bundle of bloody mucus and wrinkled skin. I say this reservedly: F's labour ended in a Caesarean. I was denied access to the operating theatre and waited in the recovery room. A nurse brought him out to me. I picked him up. As I leant over him, he opened his eyes. I was surrounded by surgical detritus and white walls. I unwrapped his sheet and saw the cord – gristle and cartilage – sticking out from his gently rising belly, his little legs and tiny clasped hands. The nurse hovered over me, slightly unsure about what I was doing. I wanted her to leave because I thought I was looking at the fulfilment of all my own longings. As a new father I was expected to feel proud and rather distant, but nevertheless, to be paternally concerned for 'mother and baby'. I wanted to feel something more than this. Like other men I knew at the time, I wanted to be a father in a different mould from my own. To look after my children, and not to become their remote provider. I had an intellectual appreciation of what I was going to undertake. K was born in May, and I'd spend the summer looking after him with F, and then, in the autumn, I'd find a job. My plans, for all their good intentions, had missed the point, and they left me entirely unprepared.

The bliss of fatherhood lasted for a couple of minutes in the mess of a post-op room. For the first two months I could find no deep feelings for him. I was supposed to love him, but his insatiable demands overwhelmed me. I looked inside myself for what I needed to provide him with emotional sustenance. I could find very little. I foraged amongst the old nursery songs and endearing phrases I recalled from my own childhood. I tried to re-imagine the warmth of my own mother's body. Most important, the memory emerged of boys who had looked after me at boarding school. It was their kind words and concern when I was homesick that provided me with the rudiments of a male language of empathy. I had no recollection of my father ever looking after me. Nothing emerged from within me of its own accord, no welling up of tenderness, no spontaneous giving over of myself. Instead what came foremost to my mind was the loss of myself. Sitting down for a few minutes of contemplation, or to read a newspaper, became impossible. Even my thoughts – the few I had left after the sleepless nights – were no longer my own.

F and I were living in a one-bedroom flat, having recently moved from the house we had briefly shared with Michael. Downstairs there lived a man in his seventies who used to weed the borders of the small back garden with a hoe. He was very slow, as if he had all the time in the world. He would gather up the weeds and put them in a Sainsbury's plastic carrier bag. Sometimes when I was in the super-market I saw him shopping. He would shop the way he gardened, musing down the aisles, studying the items he picked off the shelves, turning them over to read the labels and usually replacing them. He never bought much. Our own lives had adopted the old man's horizons of the super-market and the washeteria. We didn't seem to do much either. The rhythms of the day were organized around shop-ping, eating and looking after K. It was like beginning one's own life over again – the immobility, a sense of one's time not being one's own. For the first few months the outside world went into abeyance. I experienced fatherhood as being cast adrift in a timeless and unstructured existence and yet I had never felt more restrained, my days shrunk to a single room and a bucketful of nappies and an unsleep-ing baby. We went to bed at nine o'clock each night. What appeared to an outside observer to be a closed, still world was not dissimilar to Doctor Who's Tardis. It contained an extraordinary intensity of living, an implosion of time and space.

I railed against all this. Even as I wanted it, I sought to impose my order on it and bring boundaries and a timetable to this amorphous, ghostly family schema. Unlike my own father's role, which had a clearly defined purpose in his work, my attempt to find another identity as a father left me flailing about in the place where the borders between what was me and not me, home and work, feminine and masculine had become confused. I wanted to look after a baby at home, not as a mother but as a man. As a father my task was to enable my son, as he grew, to identify with my masculinity and separate himself from his mother. Would I not confuse him by adopting a feminine position?

72

Was my wish for this reversal of roles a simple over-identification with my own mother, a pathological symptom of my failure to differentiate myself from her? At the time I didn't know how to ask myself these questions but they were implicit in the way in which I tried to cope with the contradictions. On a more banal level, society expected a man to support his wife and his child by working for his living. If he failed to do this it was a sign that he was weak, or incapable. My masculine identity, and the language with which I was both familiar and competent, crumbled into pathos, and it felt as if there was nothing to replace it with.

My intention of finding a job a few months after K's birth was delayed until the autumn and then beyond. By the time K was one year old, F had enrolled at university and I remained at home for the next three years to look after him. I was able to do this because I learnt from F how to give my time and attention. I could never have managed this alone. I think it was her own early years with her sisters, so different from my own childhood, that offered me a model. Something in the experience of girlhood, in the detail of concern about one's own life and the life of others, enables a sense of empathy to develop. In my own boyhood I always looked beyond myself and ignored or denied feelings which might hinder my progress through life. I was oblivious to the small details that make up the giving and receiving of comfort and pleasure in relationships, and when I was faced with them, I believed them to be superfluous and 'in the way'.

Looking after K was like an act of reparation, a rebuilding

of my own unfinished childhood through the life of another. I used to take him to the One o'Clock Club in Finsbury Park, where he pottered from one toy to another while I chatted with the other parents, mostly young mothers, about children's things. Once or twice a week I looked after other toddlers in return for their mothers taking care of K. There was something safe about this world of regularity, of small, intimate details. After the trauma of the early months I no longer hankered for a return to the past. But my confinement with a small child at home, with its invisible achievements and lack of recognition, left me feeling purposeless and frustrated. Much as I enjoyed being with small children, I also wanted to work. The problem with the idea of role reversal is that it pitches men into the very social isolation women had been struggling to escape from. As K turned increasingly to the world outside, so did I.

I thought, when I began writing this, that I would find it relatively straightforward to return to these early days. But I don't. I had assumed that it would be enough to describe my difficult transition into parenthood. I could then pass on to its pleasures: the sensuality of holding a small child's body, the unconditional love, the security of habit, the visits to the park; the intimacy of the conversations with other parents as we discussed illnesses, clothes, food, problems; the excitement of his first words, his first steps, and his first pair of shoes when he bounced like a kangaroo in the Clarks shoe shop; the nights, the three of us sleeping in the same bed together; the play and the mess. And then later, when time had ceased to be interminable and the hours and the days passed at a more normal pace

74

and the outside world reasserted itself, the realization of how short this span of life was to be. The maelstrom of early parenthood passing, and a dawning of time on one's hands, of being left alone again with one's own life. And a feeling of something close to bereavement. I had imagined this would suffice, and it would be what I would write about. But it is not the whole story. There is already plenty written on the subject. There are enough self-help manuals, personal reminiscences and academic surveys on fatherhood to fill a bibliography a dozen pages long. But the means of talking about a father's love are still limited. Men are expected to speak of being fathers in terms of possessive pride or to be sentimental and nostalgic. Yet there is much more to say.

When my son was four I began to work as a freelance journalist. One day I was on the phone when K reached up to the receiver and tried to pull it out of my hand. If he was unwell, I would sit at the table holding him while I wrote. When it came to using two hands for a typewriter I had to endure his pained attempts to win over my attention. I found myself increasingly reasserting my own life against his. I wanted a distance between us. It was a conflict between my need for him and his need for me. He could not be a party of my new-found activities and he felt that exclusion. He fought to get back in, and I, guilty and resentful, pushed him away. I think now, in retrospect, that it is this struggle – not just for his independence from me, but mine from him – that makes it difficult to dwell on this time. It feels shameful to admit to such petty but desperate tussling with a four-year-old. I began to look forward to the day he would start school, and when he finally did, and the three of us stood in his new classroom, I felt a period of my life had come to an end and I wondered why I had ever wished it to be over. What he gave to our relationship in those early years had often gone unrecognized by me, because it had been intangible and immeasurable. Our love had been unequal. Love is essentially narcissistic. We use our beloved to satisfy a need within us. It is the same with children, except that we are supposed to love them in order to let them go. Only it is never quite so straightforward. I wonder, what feelings do fathers satisfy when they love their sons?

Anatole Mallarmé, the second son of the French Symbolist poet Stéphane Mallarmé, having been dangerously ill for some months, died on 6 October 1879; he was eight years old. On that day Mallarmé had written to his friend Montesquiou: 'I am quite beside myself, like someone on whom a terrible and endless wind is blowing. All night vigils, contradictory emotions of hope and sudden fear have supplanted all thoughts of repose.' When he returned home from posting his letter he found his son was dead. He was inconsolable. In August he had written to Henry Ronjon that the thought of his son's death 'was too much for me: I cannot bring myself to face this idea.' And now he had to, and in an attempt to accept his loss he decided to write about his son. He would write him back into life and fill the void the small boy had left with beautiful words and images. Only he was unable to, and could only manage halting fragments of poems.

you can, with your little
hands, drag me
into the grave – you
have the right –
– I
who follow you, I
let myself go –
– but if you
wish, the two
of us, let us make . . .

an alliance
a hymen, superb
– and the life
remaining in me
I will use for —

and no mother
then?

Mallarmé cannot master his son's death with words. He
cannot muster them into any sense. He is haunted by dreams
of his own extinction. He calls upon his son for an alliance
to rescue him from this dark hole of loss. He reasons that
the little boy had no conception of death and therefore
cannot know he is dead, and so he has not died. Mallarmé
clings to his syllogistic juggling in order to keep his son's
memory alive. All he has is language and it utterly fails
him. He is wombless. Without the capacity to reproduce
life, he can only hope, in the face of nothingness, to remake
his son's life in a denial of his death.

And dreams of filiation
that is masculine, dreams
of God the father
issuing from himself
in his son – and
no mother then.

Mallarmé is expressing a wish similar to that of Words-
worth, whose sentiment 'the child is father to the man'
helped to originate the metaphor of the 'inner child'. The
creation of a man's life is to be found within himself. In
fatherhood, he attempts to recreate the child he once was
with his son. The small boy provides him with a love in
an alliance against women, without whom the worldly pain
of loss and bereavement – even death – can be evaded.

The Romantic notion of the inner child has become a part
of English popular culture. *Peter Pan* celebrated boyhood and
boyishness, and in the United States, Walt Disney, with
his prurient disavowal of sexuality and conservative attitude
to motherhood and femininity, embraced its whimsical boy-
worship. One of Elvis Presley's best known songs, 'You
Gave Me a Mountain', reflects this preoccupation with a
man's longing for a son.

The song is a sentimental ballad about a man who has
retreated from the adult world of sexuality and relationships.
Women are the cause of his pain and only the presence
of his son offers him any consolation. Presley repeats this
sentiment in the song 'My Boy', in which a man's son is
the only thing of value in a marriage which has failed. Both
are songs of reparation in which the son offers the father

hope of rebirth. The male longing is for a literal son, a real person, but it is also an attempt to regenerate a self-love, a substitute for the lost narcissism of childhood – and for the son he once wished to be, a boy who was loved to completeness by his mother.

In the late 1980s Hollywood cinema became preoccupied with fatherhood, perhaps best exemplified in the 1987 box-office hit *Three Men and a Baby*. With the growing incidence of divorce the underlying concern was with the status of fathers and their rights over their children. In his book *Hollywood from Vietnam to Reagan* Robin Woods identified the 'restoration of the father' as the dominant project of contemporary Hollywood. Films such as Steven Spielberg's *Hook* and Terry Gilliam's *The Fisher King* began a critique of an acquisitive, work-oriented, self-centred masculinity: the spontaneity and sensuality of the small boys men once were had, they believed, been repressed and forgotten in the pursuit of selfish ambition. Men, unable to relate to themselves, and consequently to their children, had become emotionally inept and unqualified for fatherhood, responding to their sons and daughters as if they were sibling rivals. Both films were responses to the problems men were facing with women and in their family life. Both star Robin Williams, who has used his acting career to highlight the debate about a father's relationship with his children. He has brought to the screen a representation of boyishness which reveals not just his ambiguous view of women, but wider questions about the nature of a father's love.

Hook is a maudlin and reactionary reworking of J. M. Barrie's *Peter Pan*. Robin Williams plays the now grown-up

Peter Pan, who is a successful and wealthy lawyer but a negligent and inconsiderate father. He has earned the contempt and disappointment of his young son, and the scorn of his daughter. Unaware of his past identity, both his children are kidnapped by Hook, who has come from Neverland to the London home of their grandmother Wendy to seek his revenge on Pan. The adult Peter Pan is confronted by Tinkerbell, who tells him that he must rediscover within himself the innocence and zest of the boy he once was. 'I know why I grew up,' he says at one point; 'because I want to be a father.' He has become a father, but in the process has lost touch with his own boyhood.

The adult Pan meets the Lost Boys and struggles to regain his ability to fly. When he has finally defeated Hook and rescued his son, he tells the boy the happy thought which helped him to fly again; it was 'you'. The bond between father and son has been asserted. Pan asks his children for one happy thought to help them fly back home. His daughter says 'Mummy', his son says 'my dad'. Pan has won back his children's love, and in the process he has re-established his dominance within his family. Even the children's happy thoughts reflect the hierarchy of the middle-class nuclear family. The little girl's response 'Mummy' lacks an article, and is a passive identification which suggests that 'Mummy' is something she is always destined to be a part of. In contrast, the boy lays claim to his father – '*my* dad' – an active assertion of his inheritance. In *Hook* a father's love is indivisible from his authority within his family. Behind its sentimental depiction of the adult Peter Pan emerging from his prolonged emotional adolescence, there lies an ideological reassertion of men's paternal rights over women and children.

In *The Fisher King* Williams plays Parry, an academic whose wife is murdered by a man who has been goaded into a random act of violence by a radio talk-show host called Jack. Parry's loss catapults him into a catatonic state, and he ends up living on the street like a modern-day Holy Fool. His recovery begins following a chance encounter with Jack, who has seen the error of his selfish ways and has also hit rock bottom. This romance of male friendship is based on the Arthurian legend of the Fisher King, known also as the Maimed King, the guardian of the Holy Grail who has been wounded in battle by a spear thrust through both his thighs. His wounds refuse to heal and his life is reduced to a state of bereavement. Only a knight who is able to travel through the barren lands of the 'wailing women' can rescue him from his predicament. Jack must confront and accept his own need and the emotional demands of his lover, Ann, in order to save Parry. The film is about men coming to terms with their need for women, and in particular with 'the original wound' of the loss of their mother. Parry's awakening from his catatonic state suggests he can now mourn his wife and so regain his life. Despite the film's liberal attitude to men's feelings, its treatment of the women is conservative. Women's love is crucial for the men's recovery. Women nurture them back to life and represent the Grail's promise of the fulfilment of men's desire. But the women are excluded from the men's rebirth, which is symbolically played out beneath the moon in Central Park. Between the men, recumbent and naked on the grass, lies a wooden Pinocchio doll Jack has given Parry. Pinocchio had no mother: he was created by a man.

At a time when men perceive themselves to be ailing, the predicament of the 'wounded men' in Williams's films is seen as being a consequence of a patrimony in crisis. Men's sexual virility is waning and fathers have lost touch with their sons. Williams's films, ostensibly liberal interpretations of the condition of masculinity, nevertheless promote fatherhood and male friendship as a defence against women. They finally denigrate or at least displace women, in the process of trying to regenerate a damaged and impotent male sexuality.

This crisis of fatherhood has been evident in the number of domestic sieges in Britain. These have been documented by Roland Littlewood and Maurice Lipsedge, whose findings were published in the journal *Anthropology and Medicine* in June 1997. They typically involved a young father who had been estranged from his partner and deprived of access to his children. These domestic sieges were twice as likely as criminal sieges to end in the death or wounding of the hostages. In eight of the nineteen cases analysed the hostage-taker died. This compared to no deaths in thirty-nine comparable criminal sieges. According to Littlewood and Lipsedge, the domestic sieges lasted an average of seventeen hours, during which a crowd would gather to listen to the father's appeals for justice. Two weeks after I read this report there was a small news item in the *Guardian* detailing the suicide of a father. The man had first battered his wife with a baseball bat before driving his two sons, aged one year and three years, to Beachy Head. He had parked his car and then jumped off the cliff with them. It reminded me of other cases in which men whose marriages were falling apart had murdered their children before committing suicide – as if the thought of the children surviving alone with their mother was more unbearable than their deaths; or perhaps these men were terrified of dying on their own. Or perhaps it was a simple act of revenge against the woman – an act of sudden precipitate madness. A father may be willing to die for his children, but he may also be ready to kill them to avoid losing their love. These are extreme cases but they reveal the precariousness of men's relationships with their families. Like Williams's screen personae they reflect the continuing uncertainty about what it means to be a father.

The language which maintained the father as a symbol of transcendence and authority is dead. In recent years we have seen a plethora of images of beautiful young men cuddling babies, but there are precious few images of the ordinariness of a loving father. I have found one in a poem called 'Dawn at St Patrick's' by the Irish poet Derek Mahon. He has spent Christmas in St Patrick's psychiatric hospital in Dublin. He watches the last planes of the year pass overhead and imagines the home he will soon be returning to:

> as I chew my thumb
> and try to figure out
> what brought me to my present state –
> an 'educated man', a man of consequence, no bum
> but one who has hardly grasped what life is about,
> if anything. My children, far away,
> don't know where I am today,

in a Dublin asylum
with a paper whistle and a mince pie,
my bits and pieces making home from home.
I pray to the rain-clouds that they never come
where their lost father lies; that their mother thrives;
     and that I
may measure up to them
before I die.

Mahon's modest wish to show personal integrity and to be a good father does not add up to a blueprint for a new patrimony. But in his humble recognition of his own failings and of what is important to him, he offers a compassion and empathy for his children. A father's love.

4

NEW MEN

A man must partly give up being a man
With womenfolk.

ROBERT FROST

I

I have a copy of the *Sun* in front of me, dated 10 July 1997. Its headline reads A BITTER DIVORCE. 'Sandra Elloway called time on her marriage to boozy husband Michael by serving divorce papers on him in the PUB.' On page four there is a series of snapshots depicting her husband in repose on a sofa, a bed, a sunbed; 'he's crashed out and sleeping off the drink'. 'Most of our marriage has been a complete waste of time,' Sandra Elloway told the *Sun*. 'He's got no interest in the kids. He falls in with his cronies and spends all his time with them. I've had enough.' Some months later the *Sun* ran a front-page story about Emma Morgan, who divorced her soccer-mad husband Kevin because he loved Manchester United more than her. She said: 'When I told Kev I was leaving he showed no pain . . . when Cantona left United he cried like a baby.' Kevin admitted she was right: 'I suppose It's funny how football affects some men. I live for it.' He confessed that he had feelings for his wife and children but that they could never compete with Old Trafford. These stories are not simply salacious tabloid gossip; they reflect a widespread uncertainty about the durability of relationships between men and women.

When my son was small, many of the women with children I knew were single mothers. Isolated and with no money to spend on anything apart from the basics, they had the gruelling task of looking after a small child alone. One friend of mine, exhausted and at her wits' end, shut her three-year-old son in his bedroom one afternoon in a desperate attempt to stop herself harming him. To make sense of what's happening in family life, and to men and women's relationships, it is necessary to talk about wider economic and social forces. The problem goes beyond the individual. Women's expectations have been transformed in the last thirty years. They want something more from the men in their relationships. A growing number of women have achieved financial independence and have become self-reliant. They want companionship, but find it only with their female friends. They're on their own because they believe they will lose their hard-won freedom in a relationship with a man. Everything about and between men has been called into question. Our work, the nature of our sexuality, the ideals of manliness are all changing. The conventional idea of marriage, where a wife lends emotional support to a working husband, is giving way to more equitable, diverse and flexible forms, founded on trust and intimacy. In theory at least, there is no longer any prescribed role for a man or a woman: either one may go out to work, look after the children, do the shopping, use contraception. According to *Social Trends*, 27 (1997), the government's annual survey of the population, less than half of adults in Britain will be married in twenty years' time. Work has given women a greater degree of financial independence and the opportunity to exercise more choice in their lives. Large numbers have been ending their marriages. In the UK in 1993 two and a half times more divorces were granted to women than to men. Over half the divorces granted to wives were for a husband's unreasonable behaviour. If this trend continues, 40 per cent of all recent marriages will end in divorce. Men are finding it difficult to adapt to women's rising expectations and women are disappointed and angry. Women blame men for failing to be good fathers, for failing to express themselves in relationships and for the lacklustre nature of their companionship. Men are losing their position as head of household and must renegotiate their relationships with women and children on the basis of a new kind of equality. But they don't know how to respond: they fall into ready compliance, they portray themselves as hapless victim, they hit back, or they resort to the traditional strategy of men faced with irate women and turn on the TV or go out for a drink. But when it comes to relationships men are lost for words.

We cannot just rely on apportioning personal blame or on moral exhortations for individual men to improve. The problems men and women face in their relationships are part of a wider, historical change in family life. The 1960s was the golden age of capitalism, and the family was the principal site of consumption. My father, usually indifferent to popular culture, brought home the Beatles' single 'I Wanna Hold Your Hand'. We were part of the new consumerism of the time: a car, Tupperware, nylon sheets, washing machine, coffee, Coca-Cola and television. There was sufficient money for my mother to pursue the new fashions, to bring into our home the new designs and decor. Family life was beginning to change as consumer culture swept through the front doors of our suburban homes, weakening the status of women as homemakers and mothers. Consumerism encouraged individual choice. New liberal divorce laws were introduced and contraception became widely available. Women began to sense that they need no longer remain wives and mothers; however, their new desire for independence continued to be obstructed by sex discrimination. By the end of the 1960s many middle-class families were beset by an ambivalence over the role of women and the nature of femininity. My two sisters were expected to do well at school and make good careers for themselves. They were also expected to marry and become mothers and housewives.

The culture of choice and individuality precipitated the contradiction in women's lives between being a housewife and mother and pursuing new opportunities in work and education. On the other hand it confirmed men's traditional roles. Albert Finney in *Saturday Night and Sunday Morning* (1960) ushered in the 1960s with the single-minded purpose of having a good time. In 1963 James Bond came to the screens with the release of *Dr No*, mixing ambition and violent machismo with the pursuit of women. *Penthouse* and *Playboy* catered for the man-about-town in search of pleasure. The sexual revolution of the 1960s promoted men's sexual freedom and personal status without any accompanying change in their roles. Nevertheless, the permissive climate enabled women to begin to express their own sexuality, and to make new demands in their marriages and relationships. By the 1970s men, particularly the educated middle-class, were under pressure to change their attitudes towards women and to accept their share of childcare and housework. Men experienced this crisis in their identities through women, in the form of broken relationships and divorce. Victor Seidler, a sociologist, recalled the time and sounded an apocalyptic warning: 'I recognise that something is terribly wrong but I don't know what to do about it. I'm shaken by the fury and the bitterness. I find it hard to accept that things can be that bad, though I know that at some level they are. Part of me just wants to flee or withdraw. It is as if all long term heterosexual relationships in our time are doomed.'

The growth of the women's and gay liberation movements during this time began a dramatic reappraisal of family life, sexuality and relationships. People's expectations of marriage changed. The notions of submitting oneself to duty and service were overtaken by the new ideals of personal intimacy and happiness. Experts began to encourage people to express their feelings towards one another. As men and women aspired to personal fulfilment, the expression and acknowledgement of emotions began to overtake conventional marriage roles. The institution of marriage cannot guarantee the success of these new ideals and it has been superseded by what the academic Anthony Giddens has termed the 'pure relationship'. Intimacy between men and women is no longer supported by an affirming institution. Instead a couple must continually replenish their relationship through discussion and self-analysis in order to make it 'work'. The reward is emotional satisfaction. But this is a nebulous and transitory experience, and it can lead to constant and renewed demands on a partner. In a society in which so much is uncertain, where individuals are looking for stability, love has become a secular religion which promises to provide a lifetime's emotional satisfaction, fulfil all our hopes and banish loneliness and despair. Love and intimacy can become a tyrannical pursuit of happiness.

Personal relationships have become our modern obsession. I used to watch the Saturday night TV programmes *The Other Half* and *Love Me Do*, in which 'three engaged couples play to win the wedding of their dreams'. I have a barely suppressed interest in listening in to the relationships of other people and these programmes were an invitation to hear the contestants' confessions. Nestling together on a settee in *The Other Half*, couples acted out the clichés of love, the man with his arm around his wife, she nestling into his protective embrace. There was something excruciating about this parody of romance, but for all their exuberance and excess, these game shows are an indication that we are increasingly committed to the 'pure relationship'. In spite of ourselves, we want to compare and contrast the relationships of these strangers with our own. The winners were the couples with a sufficient appreciation of one another and their friends to guess correctly the things they might say and do. It is a form of emotional knowledge – an understanding of oneself and the moods and temperaments of others – which is a pre-eminent asset in establishing and sustaining relationships. These game shows were a way of testing our own understanding of this knowledge. Perhaps this also explains the endurance of Cilla Black's *Blind Date*, which presents a mixture of salacious gossip and speculation about people's relationships. The popularity of TV programmes such as *Heartbreak High*, *Friends* and *This Life*, in which characters test out this emotional knowledge, reflects its importance in the lives of young people. The large number of young, unmarried men and women choosing to live alone is giving rise to a growing singles culture. For the generation who were children and teenagers in the 1980s, there are few certainties about marriage.

Geoff Deane, writing in a 1990 issue of *Options* magazine, lamented men's fate in the coming decade. 'Let me welcome you to the thirty-something Utopia. For many the nineties will herald an emotional Armageddon. Divorced, defunct and unfashionable to boot.' And many men found that he was right. The transition to a service economy in the 1980s had led to the decline of traditional industries: millions of men were made redundant. In the 1990s the scythe of economic deregulation swept through the banking and service sectors in the South of England, precipitating unemployment and insecurity amongst the middle classes. Men felt a relative decline in their status and social prestige. The search for profit and the cuts in the public services led to the reorganization of workplaces and the redefinition of job descriptions. Careers became short-term contracts, free-lancing, part-time work and piece-work at home. Throughout the post-war golden age of the consumer society men's lifelong careers had underpinned the middle-class nuclear family and its twenty-five-year mortgage. According to Will Hutton, writing in the *Guardian* in 1995, by the year 2000 it will have become a minority form of work. With negative equity on their mortgages, falling salaries and pressure to increase personal productivity, men were forced to work longer hours. In 1996 the recruitment agency Austin Knight reported that two thirds of men were working more than forty hours a week and a quarter more than fifty hours. In the same year the Family Policy Studies Centre in their booklet *Parenting in the 1990s* argued that middle-class fathers were working longer hours than ever and played relatively little part in the care of their children. Already under pressure from women to reform their emotional lives, the generation of thirty- and forty-something men who had inherited their fathers' expectations of a career for life, were faced with the prospect of remorseless work and the constant threat of redundancy. A decade earlier, in 1987, I interviewed Tim Kemp, a training consultant, for a newspaper article. He told me, 'Men use work in the same way we use clothing. It's not just status we're looking for; it's an identity. Without work men feel they have lost their place in the world – they have become non-people.' Whatever happened to the New Man, with his concern for his children and family life?

II

It was around 1984 that I started to work as a freelance journalist. Journalism provided me with the opportunity to witness the changes taking place in the 1980s. Beggars were just beginning to appear on the streets. Money had found a new breed of spender, able to justify the pursuit of his or her personal pleasure in the face of growing poverty. The consumer market was booming. Popular culture was full of verve; it encouraged ambition. As politicians and the media trumpeted the end of the class system and everyone declared themselves classless, a new class system was emerging to continue the transformations in family life that had begun in the 1960s.

In 1987 Kevyn Jones, then chairman of Mothercare, made an intuitive guess that men's relationships with their families were changing. He noticed an increasing number of young fathers out Saturday shopping and pushing the buggy, and so he featured men in the Mothercare catalogue. In the summer edition the 'New Man' was on the front cover. On page 161 he was changing a nappy and on page 171 he was bathing the baby. I phoned Mothercare and was told by their spokeswoman, Sally Olliver, 'Men aren't ashamed to come into our stores any more; we're reflecting that's happening in the family.' Bob Geldof broke another convention and became the first man to appear on the front cover of *Cosmopolitan* – with his young daughter. Even Prince Charles was given the title 'New Father'. And the ad for Oxo, the nation's favourite, introduced a husband and father who knew his way around a kitchen. People *felt* that men were changing. Women's magazines began to commission articles on masculinity and male sexuality. The New Man was being invented by anecdote, inspired guesswork and wishful thinking. There was precious little evidence of his existence. In 1983 the Equal Opportunities Commission had published *Fathers, Childbirth and Work*, a survey on men's attitudes to paternity leave: 282 fathers-to-be were questioned – 91 per cent wanted a scheme similar to maternity leave, but there was little enthusiasm for any prolonged period at home; only eight men wanted a leave of eight weeks or more. The great majority – 207 – were evenly divided between one and two weeks. Four years later a report, *Inside the Family*, published by the Family Policy Studies Centre, commented that the 'New Man' was charac-terized by his 'rebuttal of the traditional images and pursuits of "macho man". Thus "New Man" is caring and demonstra-tive, slightly narcissistic, liberated and very laid back.' The authors could find little evidence of his increased involve-ment in childcare and housework, but they concluded that 'the family today reflects dimensions of both change and continuities'.

Popular culture is a useful indicator of changing attitudes. Back in 1979 *Cosmopolitan* had launched *Cosmo Man*, a maga-zine for its substantial but covert male readership. It failed to find a market. Men who read their wives', girlfriends' or sisters' copy of *Cosmopolitan* were unwilling to buy a maga-zine about themselves, and after a couple of issues it was closed down. In 1988 I interviewed Linda Kelsey, then editor of *Cosmopolitan*, for an article about the market for

men's magazines. Reflecting on the failure of *Cosmo Man*
she told me, 'We thought that men had changed as quickly
as women and that the time was right to offer them a
magazine which would discuss sex, relationships, emotions,
clothes and grooming without embarrassment. But we were
wrong.' By the mid 1980s magazine publishers were aware
that a new male consumer market was emerging, particularly in the South of England, where the retail sector of the
economy was booming. British menswear, which had tended
to conform to tribal, class cultures, was discovering a more
acquisitive and individualistic masculinity, concerned with
self-presentation and body-consciousness. There was a growing demand amongst men for *haute couture* and toiletries.
Nick Kamen, stripping off his 501s in the launderette in
the initial Levi jeans ad, launched a more sexualized image
of the male body. Outside Warren Street tube station I
picked up a copy of the free London magazine *Girl About
Town*, in which a journalist had written: 'For a lot of people
last year's advertising campaign came as a revelation – or
should that read revolution. Gone were the product shots,
naff jingles and predictable copy lines – instead we had
fetish, flesh, fulsome torsos. Those jeans, that flesh, that
man. Hey wait a minute . . . yes, but it's true, even for us
blokes Levis was one hell of a shock.' Kamen's homoerotic
body catapulted 501s into the mainstream. In a direct challenge to the traditional rules about who is looked at, straight
men were given permission to admire other men's bodies
and clothes. The relaxing of men's anxiety about being
subject to the appreciative gaze of others was part of a wider
change in attitude. The economic recession of the 1980s,

which had destroyed the old industrial base of the country, also undermined the segregation of home and work in men's lives. Men's traditional work-based cultures, which had promoted the work ethic and emotional restraint, were giving way to lifestyle and leisure activities, such as shopping.

In 1986 *Arena* magazine took advantage of this trend and established itself as the first successful men's lifestyle magazine. Its young fashion models drew on gay culture, while its articles retained a traditional masculine focus on money, style and success. *Cosmopolitan*, followed by *Options* and *Elle*, produced supplements for their male readership. Marcus Van Ackerman, editor of *Elle pour Homme*, explained the changes: 'Younger men aren't afraid to look at themselves any more. They're less likely to follow the crowd.' In metropolitan areas modish, more sensuous images of British masculinity were appearing. However, the New Man remained an elusive figure. When I asked Steve Taylor, a member of *Arena*'s original editorial group, about the new interest in male emotions, he commented, 'Sexual politics doesn't appeal to any of us. I think it would be really yuck to have a *Cosmo Man* style. Talking to men about their feelings would be a commercial death wish.' And Penny Vincenzi, then in charge of the more up-market supplement *Options for Men*, shared his view. 'Our philosophy is about power and success, getting on and making money. It's not about emotions and being a better husband.' *Practical Parenting* produced a special section for fathers in its November 1989 edition, only to announce in its editorial that the new, involved father was a myth. Its editor, Davina Lloyd, wrote that 'Men are as little involved in day to day care of their children as they were twenty years ago.' When Janice Winship asked Linda Kelsey, in an interview in September 1987, if she could characterize the new 'Cosmo man', she replied, 'I haven't really met him.'

'Well, that's an interesting confession!'

'Well I do know a few but they're very few and far between.'

In the same year I was asked to write about a telephone survey conducted by *Cosmopolitan*'s new supplement *Cosmo Man*. Five hundred men aged between twenty and thirty-five were interviewed about their attitudes towards women, sex and relationships. The survey lacked scientific rigour, but the article concluded that 'in general younger men especially have a greater respect for women's equality. They're more aware of women's sexuality than expected, and feel less threatened by it. They display a positive attitude toward working women. They are romantic, want to fall in love, and most say they want to marry and have children.' The findings are anodyne, but they illustrate the degree of change in masculinity during the late 1980s. Men's sensibilities were more self-conscious and female friendly, but all the evidence continued to confirm that there had been only a marginal increase in their participation in housework and childcare. The group with the lowest involvement were married men with young children. The December issue of *Options for Men* carried an interview with the playwright Alan Bleasdale which typified the contradictory nature of the New Man. 'I don't wash up and that. I suppose it's another sign of working-class thuggery. In that sense I am not a New Man. But in my relationships I am. I talk, I discuss my emotions. I am very tactile with my children. And I cry.'

By the end of the decade journalist Angela Phillips had delivered her judgement on the New Man. She remarked that he had 'swapped his jeans for a designer suit, stopped pretending to share the childcare and got heavily into the new culture of cash'. She cited a book, *Give and Take in Families* by Julian Brannen and Gail Wilson, published in 1987, which analysed the distribution of income within the family. In their survey they found that 50 per cent of fathers in joint income families contributed nothing towards the cost of childcare. In December 1993 the marketing organization Mintel International published *Women 2000*, a report which appeared to support Angela Phillips's verdict. Its survey of 1500 men and women found that fewer than one in ten women thought her partner shared the cooking equally, compared to two men in ten who thought they did. And while eight out of ten women agreed that they took or shared equally all major financial decisions, fewer than four in ten had their own bank account. Mintel's consumer manager Angela Hughes declared: 'Men seem to set out with good intentions to share the domestic chores but the catalyst appears to be the arrival of children. At this stage, the man appears to abdicate responsibility for his share, regardless of whether his partner is working.' In August of the same year the National Child Development Study, which is following the lives of 11,500 men and women born in one week in March 1958, presented its ten-yearly report to the British Association meeting at Keele University. The generation of thirty-three-year-olds, it stated, had no great faith in marriage. Only one in ten agreed that married people were generally happier. The authors argued that women continued to bear the weight of family responsibilities and that marital breakdowns were creating a new underclass of women who were trapped in poverty. They could find little evidence of the New Man: 'There are few signs that men had metamorphosed into the caring and labour-sharing breed that the media was trumpeting in the early 1990s.'

It was difficult to gauge the changes in masculinity in the 1980s. In my experience, the media employed the term New Man on the basis of rumour, supposition and anecdote. An editor knew of a friend's husband or brother who looked after his children. Another felt intuitively that something about men was changing. I was sent on an assignment to interview men who had swapped roles with their wives and were looking after their children at home. My first encounter was with a successful freelance journalist who was ensconced in his study while the full-time nanny looked after his child downstairs. He proceeded to give me a detailed account of this woman's failings, coming to the conclusion that they – and by this he really meant his wife, who was in full-time work – would have to find a replacement. My second contact was a man looking after two children in a small flat in South London. His wife was a social worker. He was in his middle forties and his children were aged eighteen months and three years. He found it difficult, particularly because they were short of money. He'd given up his job, but he had no regrets. He told me he 'loved' what he was doing.

The changes in men's lives were intangible and hard to

quantify because they took place in their emotional being and in the quality of their relationships. The consumer market and new patterns of work played their part, but the most significant influence was the shifting attitudes of women. It was women who were campaigning for flexitime, part-time work, job-sharing and parental leave. For the same assignment I had interviewed Jim Bewsher, an official with the old public services union NUPE, who commented: 'Union officials are full-time and male. We inhabit a culture where job sharing is an alien idea. If full-time officials were offered part-time work they'd take it as an affront to their masculinity. It would suggest that they couldn't cope with their workload.' His opinion was supported by Tim Kemp: 'The few men that I've met working flexitime have viewed it as an opportunity to avoid traffic jams rather than fit in child care arrangements – men are going to have to realise that achieving a more equal and fair society will mean giving up power.' The New Man was a response to women's desire for change, but there was also a reaction amongst men to the challenge women presented.

The Big Bang of October 1985, when the City of London's financial institutions were deregulated, unleashed another kind of mythical New Man associated with champagne bars, cell phones and vast salaries. The yuppie represented a public assertion of male privilege. It was similar in the world of the media, where everyone wanted to make it, to be the individual star that would outshine all the others. Most of us were polite and circumspect in our ambition and the brasher and more brazen opportunists were frowned upon and declared too much. In the inimitable

style of the English middle classes, self-interest was disguised in a masquerade of liberal niceties. Yet the new
culture of ambition encouraged an acquisitive and go-
getting masculinity more attuned to power and money than
to children and domestic life. In the wake of the yuppie
came his more brazen and classless hybrid, the lager lout.
Reports of young men rampaging through the market towns
of Chard, Taunton and High Wycombe created a national
moral panic about a resurgence of male violence and inciv-
ility, the roots of which go back to the Falklands War.

F and I were staying in Lyme Regis over Easter 1982.
We went to Axminster for the day as the local regiment
embarked for Southampton. Lines of slow-moving troop-
carriers, lorries and jeeps wound through the narrow streets
of the town as if it were a set for the film *The Longest Day*.
The sense of unreality didn't last. The departure of the task
force triggered a jingoism cultivated by both tabloid and
broadsheet newspapers. The leader of the *Daily Mail* blasted:
'Men who can out-yomp the enemy are men with the stam-
ina and spirit to win. Boots and guts. There is still no
substitute for them.' The war was an opportunity to recover
the time when men walked tall. The *Observer* ran a story
on Prince Andrew headed HOW THE PLAYBOY PRINCE
BECAME A MAN. Peter McKay in the *Daily Express* wrote,
'Cut the girl talk, there has in the past few days been an
outbreak of nostalgia for men as brutes ... Right now it
must be quite hard to be a feminist.' And Joe Ashton, the
'Voice of the People' in the *Daily Star*, declared that what
young men on the front line thought about more than premature, violent death was 'CRUMPET, grub and CRUMPET'.

On the day of the victory parade we joined a group of protesters walking through the empty streets of London. Office workers leaned out of windows watching us quizzically. It was impromptu – perhaps fifty people and a band. The music attracted a lot of attention. No one attempted to stop us, but what stays with me is the drunken shouts of soldiers doing the rounds of the pubs as we walked past Holborn. It was a frightening moment. The patriotic fervour had promoted and glorified an aggressive masculinity. It soon backfired on the tabloids and the Conservative government when young working-class men began to rampage across Europe in the wake of English football teams, smashing up bars, bellowing racist insults and drinking themselves into a state of vindictive xenophobia. In 1985 Liverpool fans ran amok through the stands at the Heysel Stadium in Brussels. The journalist Ed Vulliamy was watching: 'it was a matter for their drunken, bloodthirsty and racist "honour" that the terraces be cleared of spics and the Union Jack flown unchallenged. I saw one Liverpool fan with a tee-shirt: "Keep the Falklands British" as though he and his mates were the task force.' Imperial fantasies were revived and unleashed on the beaches of Spain and in the football stadia of the continent by swaggering Englishmen in T-Shirts bearing the inscription ENGLAND BOYS WE ARE HERE, TO SHAG YOUR WOMEN AND DRINK YOUR BEER.

Angry and resentful young men were reacting against their own impotence. Male chauvinism was not confined to Britain and was given vent in a series of Hollywood blockbusters in which muscle-bound heroes laid waste to the imagined enemies of the all-American male. In *Commando* Arnold Schwarzenegger indulged in a tongue-in-cheek parody of this hyper-masculinity. Sylvester Stallone, in *First Blood* and *Rambo: First Blood Part II*, was less playful, providing an embittered edge to his depictions of outcast and socially disenfranchised men. It was calculated that in *Part II* Rambo 'kills eight Russians and a score of Vietnamese soldiers and bombs and shoots several hundred more; *People* magazine counts forty-four dead by Rambo's hands alone, estimating an average of one murder for ever 2.1 minutes.' In Britain there was a moral panic about the rising levels of male working-class violence. The ensuing public debate attempted to lay the blame on cinema and television, which led Prince Charles to condemn their 'incessant menu of utterly gratuitous violence' when he opened the Museum of the Moving Image in September 1988. This public reaction to *First Blood* obscured what was a useful clue to the frustrations of dispossessed men, and the violence they gave rise to. The central character, John Rambo, is a Vietnam War veteran who pits himself against a whole town and an army of police and state troopers. It is a film in which action speaks louder than words. Language for Rambo is insidious because it belongs to a government which capitulated in the Vietnam War, slighted the sacrifices of his comrades, and refused to value him as an ex-Special Forces fighter. Shunned by society, he has become an aimless drifter, and at the beginning of the film he is arrested on the outskirts of the town of Hope. The pivotal scene which marks his transformation from victim to avenger occurs in the police station: here he is asked to give his name. He refuses to answer, which provokes the sadistic deputy sheriff: 'Name? . . . Your name? . . . Name! . . . Hey, you looking for trouble? You come to the right place! You're going to talk to me. I promise you're going to talk to me!' Rambo remains silent: to give his name would be to concede that he is a petty criminal.

Rambo's response to this attempt to take away his identity is to reject the treacheries of language and opt for violence. In a choreography of kicks and punches he fights his way out of the police station and into the hills, where he is transformed into an invincible enemy of injustice. Rambo's popularity amongst boys and young men lay in this fantasy of an omnipotent, righteous male. He provided them with an example of a man escaping from shame and humiliation. The betrayals and injustices he fights against are less the consequence of America's failure in the Vietnam War, and more to do with men's humiliation on the home front, where they have been dispossessed of their roles as breadwinners. The enemies which have slighted and devalued men are unemployment, divorce and women's rising expectations. There are no women in *Rambo*, but in their absence they shape men's relationships with one another. Humiliation feminizes men, and men threatened with humiliation must constantly prove their integrity by attempting to assert themselves over others. Silence combined with physical prowess speaks louder than words. Like the warmongering English press during the Falklands War, *Rambo* was attempting to turn the clock back: the traditional male virtues of physical strength, solitude and emotional restraint were replaced by violence, paranoia and social isolation. After I'd been to the film I asked an acquaintance whether he was intending to go and see it. He was a man who abhorred violence. 'No,' he answered emphatically, 'never.' When I told him that it was actually quite a good film, he repeated that he would not go and see it because he was worried he might enjoy the violence. Rambo is a male fantasy of violent retribution. He is not simply the antithesis of the New Man; he is the other side of the same coin.

III

By the mid 1980s many men who had supported the women's movement were turning to the figures of their fathers, to their own roles as fathers, and a reclamation of their male potency. Organizations like Families Need Fathers began campaigning against the divorce laws and for men's right to custody of their children. Academic papers, articles in journals and newspapers, and workshops debated the failures of fathers, parental leave schemes, role reversal, shared parenting, men's relationship to children and practical issues of childcare. Numerous popular books offered advice on becoming a new kind of involved father. By 1992 there was a ready constituency for the 'Wild Men', an import from the US, inspired by Robert Bly's book *Iron John*. While the New Man had taken his inspiration from the women's movement – rejecting the masculinity of a father and embracing his more feminine feelings – the Wild Men were intent upon reclaiming their fathers and their own male potency. For Bly, the archetypal New Man only proved that men had lost touch with their inner virility. The bond between father and son had been broken by waged work. Boys raised exclusively by their mothers had learnt to see their father through her eyes: 'If the son learns feeling primarily from the mother, then he will probably see his own masculinity from the feminine point of view as well.' Bly argued that modern men were unable to grow up and relate to women as adults. They became trapped in compliant relationships, leaving them feeling powerless and manipulated. The New Man of the 1980s is Bly's 'naive man'. He can be receptive, can feel the other's pain, but he cannot say what he wants; he is too frightened to say 'no'. According to Bly, this unmanliness represents a crisis in men's relationships with their fathers. Groups of men attended weekend gatherings in the countryside, using ritualised dancing, drum-beating and male bonding to make primeval attempts to harness their 'masculine free spirit'. The purpose of the Wild Men movement was to rediscover the father within and tap his power.

In the same year Norman Dennis and George Erdos published a pamphlet called *Families without Fathers* for the right-wing think-tank, the Institute of Economic Affairs. Their argument was similar to Bly's: the promiscuous values of the 1960s had weakened family morality and undermined the authority of the father. Tradition and duty were being pilloried by men evading their responsibilities as sexual partners and fathers. Culture had created an atmosphere in which 'ever-larger numbers of biological fathers – invited to be undertakers of nothing but the easy, pleasant and exciting task of sexual intercourse itself – rationally eschewed the heavy risks of responsibilities of sociological parenthood.' The authors depicted a popular culture of ingratitude and easy virtues, which had created a generation of selfish and morally weak men who have abandoned their partners and children to their fate. The authors laid the blame for the breakdown of family and fatherhood on the women's movement and the reforming ideas of the 1960s. It was a message the governing classes of first Conservative and then New Labour were ready to adopt. Their attempts to contain the personal behaviour of individuals – particularly single mothers – appeared to be an easier option than tackling the inequality and poverty which underlay many of the problems of family life.

The recurrent debates over 'family values' and the so-called 'war between the sexes' led to increasingly virulent criticism of the women's movement. The most publicized anti-feminist diatribe, *No More Sex War: The Failures of Feminism*, was published in 1992 by a journalist, Neil Lyndon. Writing in *The Sunday Times* magazine in 1991, he had declared, 'It is hard to think of one example of systematic and institutionalised discrimination against women in Britain today.' In contrast, the prologue to *No More Sex War* comprises a list of grievances which demonstrates the 'routine, systematic and institutionalised disadvantage for men': such discrimination could be seen in the denial of men's rights in custody battles, and in decisions over abortions, especially when fathers were not married. New fathers were denied paternity leave, widowers were not entitled to the same state pension as widows, and men could not be classed as dependent in claiming social security benefit. He argued that the women's liberation movement had been 'fundamentally false in logic, thoroughly false in history and poisonous in effect'.

The impact of the women's movement on his own life can be gauged by an article written by his wife, Deirdre Lyndon, which appeared in the *Daily Mail* on 21 September 1992. Her opening sentence – 'This is the book that killed my marriage' – summed up the consequence of what had become her husband's obsessive loathing of feminism: 'I kept urging Neil to temper his arguments . . . 'It's not feminists you're attacking,' I would say. 'Surely it's only militant feminists?' But it became clear that it was indeed all feminists and that, to some extent, the war was indeed being waged on women.' Neil Lyndon moved out of the family home. In trying to understand her husband's 'politics of hatred', Deirdre Lyndon suggested he had moved out because 'he needed to shed all the strands of domesticity to write this book'. She added: 'In some ways I think Neil wants to strip women of motherhood.' Deirdre Lyndon had put her finger on the primary target of the backlash against feminism: mothers and motherhood.

Men's relative loss of control over wife and children – exemplified in acrimonious disputes over custody – had encouraged a search for a scapegoat in mothers and mother-hood. But if many men were having a difficult time, women were in an even less advantageous position. By 1997 the gap between women's pay and men's pay had closed by as little as 7 per cent in twenty years. In his survey 'New Perspectives on Work in the 1990s' Jonathan Gershuny concluded: 'The role that women play as mother/housekeeper still significantly affects their career opportunities. Although the absolute number of women in the workforce has increased in recent years, they still bear the greatest burden for family care, so their promotion prospects, job security and earnings potential are still more restricted than are men's.' Approximately sixteen years after the term 'New Man' was coined, it is generally accepted that the existing division of labour between men and women is unfair. However, this consciousness has not yet brought about any significant change in the domestic roles of men and women.

.

IV

In 1988 I left journalism and went to college to study for a degree. In 1992 I began to teach at the same institution. During one seminar I introduced the subject of youth cultures and began to talk about punk rock. There was a silence, and then one student asked when punk rock had first appeared. I realized that my notion of what was youth culture was more like a history lesson to this younger generation. When Acid House generated the 'Summer of Love' in 1988, it gave birth to the rave movement and a generation of young men with quite different experiences to my own. The language of feminism and gay rights had made an impact. The cattle-market mentality of the 1970s disco scene had passed into history. Instead, unisex youth culture was presented to the readers of style magazines. Calvin Klein adverts pictured the lithe bodies of androgynous young men and women, sharing the same fragrance. On the surface young men and women appeared to be at ease with each other. Social commentators argued that the feminist battles for equality had become an anachronism in this more egalitarian culture. But the differences between the sexes were overshadowed by a more general disenfranchisement of young people from the mainstream of the economy. In 1996 young people under twenty-five made up 17 per cent of the workforce and 35 per cent of the long-term unemployed. In the same year the British Youth Council reported that 60 per cent had a disposable income of less than £50 per week. The young had borne the brunt of economic change and suffered disproportionately from low wages, poverty and poor working conditions.

In the 1990s young men developed an 'ironic' response to these pressures rather than a crude male chauvinism. *Viz* comics parodied the language of feminism. Characters like Sid the Sexist and his rampant indulgence in the worst excesses of male chauvinism provided a knowing laugh. It was irreverent humour, knocking the rather puritanical and pious anti-sexist politics of the liberal middle classes. *Viz* helped to define 'lad' culture, which established a language for young men in which women and their emotional demands could be parodied, ridiculed and neutralized by humour. Laddism was self-conscious in its jibes against female equality, but the ironical quotation marks around its misogyny were marking out a new male exclusivity designed to keep women out. Then the quotation marks faded away. The first anniversary of the lads' house magazine, *Loaded*, was in 1995. Simon Hattenstone remarked on its 'get-your-tits-out-for-the-lads-but-not-while-the-football's-on' ethos and concluded that men were confused and 'not a little moronic' about sexuality. *Loaded*'s masthead 'For men who know better' had encapsulated the *raison d'être* of laddism, knowingly debunking liberal propriety and revelling in the irresponsible and the puerile. Comedians like Rik Mayall and Ade Edmondson in *The Young Ones* and *Bottom*, Frank Skinner and David Baddiel in *Fantasy Football League*, and Martin Clunes and Neil Morrissey in *Men Behaving Badly* established the lingua franca of laddism. The laughter was directed at what men were most anxious about – women, sexual relationships and their own masculinity.

Another journalist, Peter May, writing in *New Times* journal, came to the defence of *Loaded*: 'Perhaps one of the reasons lads are revelling in childishness is because they're fed up being lectured at. There's a backlash amongst young men and young women . . . against the old feminist orthodoxy that men are to blame for everything.' On the same page Sarah Williams provides the female rejoinder. 'So who is [the New Lad]? He's a football-loving, noisy-farting, bird ogling, heavy drinking, lovable (he thinks) lout.' In her listing of the New Lad's shortcomings she emphasizes his childish reliance on his mother – he eats whatever his mother cooks him and wears what she puts out. Her criticisms are familiar. There is nothing particularly new about the New Lad. Men have often demanded from women the freedom to have fun. Implicit in such demands is men's dependency upon women and their feelings of resentment when women interfere with their enjoyment. For Peter May, the caricature of the female spoil sport is a feminist. In the old 'saucy' holiday postcards it was an overweight harridan with a rolling pin, dragging her henpecked husband home by the ear. The enmity remains the same. Men experience their emotional dependency on women as if it is women who are denying them their independence. The decline of the traditional marriage and the rise of the 'pure relationship' has left men exposed to their own personal insecurities. For the New Lad, the New Man is a figure of contempt because he epitomizes men's surrender of their personal autonomy to women. His apparent willingness to give women what they want serves to underline his sexual compliance and emotional deference. He has no sexual desire. Ending his defence of the New Lad, Peter May returns to this figure of the 1980s. 'Let's be honest, when it comes down to sex appeal, New Men were wimps.' But it is an impotence which the New Lad fears in himself – that he is a man who cannot stand up to women.

V

It's tempting to dismiss the New Man as a product of the consumer market of the 1980s. The evidence of sociological and marketing surveys points to men's continued conservatism and unwillingness to relinquish traditional roles. However, the image and idea of a New Man has remained a persistent part of popular culture for almost two decades. He is an imagined figure around whom potential manly qualities have coalesced: soft, thoughtful, emotional, open, considerate, sexy, conscious of himself without being self-engrossed; his body is sensuous rather than muscular, his clothes expressive rather than conforming. He was, for a brief period in the 1980s, the image of a self-expressive masculinity which the fashion industry wanted to sell to men. He was perceived by women as an ideal lover *and* a good father to their children, an exemplar of metropolitan, educated masculinity: articulate, health-conscious, liberal, and less driven by ambition. Despite developing into a rather sanctimonious caricature, he became a yardstick against which men's emotional behaviour and attitudes could be measured and assessed.

The New Man came about as a consequence of the changes in women's personal aspirations and identities. He was an idealized version of masculinity well suited for the 'pure relationship'. His emotional intelligence, his liking for women, his commitment to parenting and to housework – all these traits were essential if he was to cope successfully in a society moving toward sexual equality. The persistence of longevity of his image, when survey after survey refuted his existence, can be explained by his metaphorical nature. Men are being thrown back onto their own emotional resources, and many have been confronted by their dependency on women and by their persistent childhood need of their mothers. With the decline in female deference, the charade of the authoritative male collapses. The New Man personified the changes in the emotional relationships between men and women, which are difficult to measure in statistical surveys. At the same time the media frequently portrayed him as a man who lacked sexual virility, and he provoked sometimes virulent opposition in men. In this antagonism lies men's attempt to reconcile their emotional need with their sexual desire. It has become a defining problem in straight male sexuality. Men are now the sex least sure of what they want, most fearful of change and the least able to articulate the pain and stress of their predicament.

5

ROMANCE

We love an idea of our own;
in short, it is ourselves that we love.

FERNANDO PESSOA

I

From where I sit at my desk I can see only a section of the sky, lingering rain clouds, part of a tree and the roofs of two houses. Occasionally a bird flies across this tableau. My window is open and I can hear the builders working on a house behind my own. They are playing their radio loudly. I try to catch the tune. It's a pop song, a love song. I hear the line: 'She loved that man for all his life.' Wistful, melancholy, regretful. The DJ announces George Michael singing 'You Have Been Loved' and his voice disappears into a cacophony of jingles and an advert for a shopping centre. It wasn't only George Michael who had succumbed to a mood of romantic melancholy in 1997. The group Faithless had a hit with 'Don't Leave', a song which repeated this refrain, adding prefixes such as 'Where's all the love gone?'; 'You know it's never been easy to love someone like me'; 'You've got me hurting'. Cast released a single called 'I'm So Lonely' and Pete Andre had a hit with 'Lonely'. Boyz II Men entered the charts at number ten with '4 Seasons of Loneliness', which begins 'I long for the warmth of days gone by when you were mine'. And the Verve's 'The Drugs Don't Work' was a plaintive appeal from a man to his lover – 'you leave my life, I'm better off dead'. Pop songs have always been love songs of loss or beatification. Listen to the great emotional romantics of the 1960s such as Roy Orbison and Marvyn Gaye. Their love songs are soliloquies of mourning. It seems that when men are romantic they do not imagine what might become of them, but rather what has been lost to them.

Women have a literature of romance which transforms private hope into a language of relationships. However much it may invest in an excess of clichés – 'My star, my one precious star, your love shall lift me into the sky from which you came. I adore you, I worship you, but I want you' – it is an attempt to reconcile the vertiginous pleasure of sex with the commitment of an enduring relationship. Romance for straight men appears to offer no similar expression of a shared experience. It is a reclusive daydreaming which stands in for feelings we cannot speak of. Like music, it provides an important vehicle for men to experience their feelings. I was thirteen when I discovered that music provided an acceptable outlet for male emotions. Following the right band conferred kudos amongst peers and provided an excuse to display the inchoate longing of adolescence. It was 1969 and I asked my grandmother to buy me the Blind Faith LP for Christmas. I took it to school and listened to

it with my friends, shut away in one of the rooms in the
music block. Here we could set aside the problems created
by our own emotional reticence in wordless communion
with Eric Clapton and Ginger Baker. Later we would sprawl
in darkened rooms, wrapped up in ourselves while Neil
Young sang 'After the Gold Rush'. Music gave form to my
emotions. However, I could not speak about them, and so
did not properly understand them; they remained incom-
municable, locked up in a private, narcissistic world. As
teenage boys we were left bereft of words that would make
sense of our relationships. Feelings were a source of embarrassment and ridicule; love was principally the pursuit of
sex. As adult men we would be expected to show our love
by providing for the material well-being of our families. In
the meantime we could dream away our early adolescence
to the sound of music. Our romance was a search for heroic
figures who could personify this amorphous longing to
become ourselves.

Men are the central figures in women's romantic fiction;
dark, authoritative, mysterious creatures who exude sexual
allure or menace. But they're the objects of female fantasy.
We have to look carefully to find the figures of male
romance, for they appear in unexpected places. This elusive
quality stems from the ambivalence of men's romance. It's
not so different from the romantic love of gay men. Gay
male romance, once forced underground, now exhibits a
self-confidence and a sense of its own history. The writer
Simon Watney recalls his boyhood in the 1960s. 'I think
back to endless Sunday afternoons spent stretched out on
the carpet in front of the TV, watching old Hollywood

movies. All over Britain thousands of us, looking for all the world like nice little boys, our eyes blinded by tears as we watched ourselves as Greta Garbo sailing away from Sweden and from love, as Bette Davis lighting his cigarette out on the verandah under the stars.' I remember similar Sunday afternoons, sitting in front of the TV waiting for the family film, my father and I hoping for an adventure or war story, my mother and sisters for a romance. One afternoon it was *Shane*, starring Alan Ladd, the story of a retired gunslinger. He comes to the defence of Joe and Marion Starrett and their young son Joey, a farmsteading family who are resisting the encroachment of a cattle baron and his hired guns. Joey tries to persuade Shane to show him his gun. One day Shane fetches his gun, sets up a can on a nearby fence, measures his distance and fires. The noise is cataclysmic and the sound fills the screen. The can spins into the air. Joey is struck dumb. Shane has a seductive power his father lacks.

Towards the end of the film Shane leaves the homestead for the final showdown with the gunslingers. As Joey runs across the fields, chasing after him, I too felt the desire to join in his plaintive cry 'Shane, Shane'. For, like Simon Watney in his fantasy of being Greta Garbo and loved by a man, in the male romance of *Shane* I also longed to be recognized and loved by a man – a man who could fulfil my desire to become myself, who would make me complete. The subject of boys' romantic daydreams are not girls, but heroes. The hero stands beyond the boy's immediate life, a shining contrast to the ordinary, a symbol of desire and the future. In my childhood, masculine romance was embodied in the figure of the cowboy; the enigmatic, lone rider, dressed in black and carrying two Colt pistols, calmly searching for some intangible goal he is destined never to find. John Wayne, with his graceful movement and casual disdain for femininity, was the heroic embodiment of this figure. As the enigmatic and racist Ethan Edwards in John Ford's film *The Searchers*, he embarks on a five-year quest in search of his niece Debbie, who has been kidnapped by Comanche Indians. When he finally locates her, he returns her to her family. Lifting her down from his horse in front of her waiting parents, he stands framed in the doorway of their unprepossessing homestead. He looks in as they lead her inside, stepping aside to make way for Debbie's brother Martin and his fiancée, the weight of his body on his right leg, his left arm across his stomach, his left hand clasping his right elbow in an act of secular benediction to the man alone. Then he turns and walks back into the desert to the chorus of Stan Jones' song 'The Searchers'. The door closes and the film ends. As a boy, I wondered, listening to that repeated refrain 'Ride away. Ride away', where Ethan Edwards rode to. Did he just ride on for ever?

The transient nature of the hero gave an ephemeral quality to my childhood romanticism. I was never quite convinced by him; never sure what was real. My only certainty was in daydreaming. In daydreams the hero comes alive. He is the figure who saves the dreamer from peril. But his significance lies in another scenario; it is the dreamer who rescues his hero. In his gratitude, the hero looks at the dreamer and in his gaze, the dreamer recognizes that his hero truly knows and understands and loves him. It is the pleasure of loving and being loved by the father we longed to have, who we search for in other men. Hero-worship leads boys into ways of being with themselves. Boys learn about love through their daydreaming about heroes. For boys, love begins as a homoerotic and solitary concern. For heterosexual men in adulthood, love and sex are separated. In order to love women sexually, men must relinquish both their need of their mothers and their homoerotic love of men. Male romance is an expression of this loss and remains a nostalgic oblation to our boyhoods. When we speak romantically we address an imaginary beloved who is the boy we once were. The male romance is an expression of our narcissism – our love of self and our unrequited love of other men.

The man who embodied romantic love in the early 1990s was Hugh Grant in *Four Weddings and a Funeral*. Self-deprecating and modest, it was his ineptitude in love which seemed to attract women's sympathies. In the film Hugh Grant plays Charles who, along with his circle of upper-middle-class friends, is a frequent guest at society weddings. The problem for Charles is that he has never attended his own wedding. His personal crisis is his inability to find true love. Charles is a 'serial monogamist' who cannot make the commitment of marriage. He is continually thwarted by a world where true love appears to be absent. In the end, of course, he commits himself to the leading lady, Carrie. Weddings, masculinity, heterosexual union and the English way of life, all appear to be confirmed as they kiss beneath an umbrella and the credits roll. But the film leaves behind a frisson of doubt about male heterosexual love. In spite of its preoccupation with marriage, it is the relationship between Charles's two gay friends, Gareth and Matthew, which embodies true love. Their love for one another casts a light on the sexual ambivalence of the male romance.

Gareth's demise from a heart attack precipitates the funeral of the film's title. After the funeral Charles talks to Tom, the film's dimwit aristocrat, who admits that the only true love in his life was a dog he once owned. Charles doubts he will ever find love at all. Both acknowledge that Gareth and Matthew are the only individuals in their acquaintance who know what love means. This is Charles's dilemma in his search for love through marriage. The latter appears to have no relation to the former, but it is the only vehicle through which he can express it. He aspires to emulate a love between two men. In order to succeed in marriage Charles must renounce the homoerotic nature of his love. As he kisses Carrie beneath the umbrella, we wonder whether he is in love with his own desire – for himself, for other men – than with a woman.

When my uncle J died last year, several years after his brother W, W's widow L showed me a photograph of the two men sitting together on a sofa. Next to them sat a third man. These were three of my father's four brothers. My two dead uncles had been officers in the merchant navy. Six months after J's funeral my father travelled to South Africa, where W had lived, because both men had asked for their ashes to be scattered where the Atlantic Ocean meets the Indian Ocean. My father told me that the shipping company they had worked for took the small party of mourners out to sea in a tugboat. They had provided a buffet lunch, with tables and chairs set out on the open deck. As soon as they left Durban harbour they ran into a gale, and the heavy seas sent the small boat tumbling and lifting, scattering the chairs and crockery and glasses across the deck. The mourners, many of whom were elderly, had no shelter and were mercilessly soaked by the spray and compelled to cling to some immovable object in order to avoid being knocked over. The ashes were scattered with more haste than had been intended, and the gale swept them into the boundlessness of the oceans. I asked L for a copy of the picture of the three brothers because I imagined that it might portray something that had eluded me all my life. Sitting together, they appeared to be men's men: relaxed, big, they exuded self-confidence and a masculine presence that came from a lifetime of working in a man's world. I know enough about them to recognize this as romantic and biographically untrue. But looking at them sitting there watching the camera, two of them dead, I felt a sense of loss out of all proportion to my actual relationship to them. I think I was taken with the idea that through them I might find a link to the manly world they had once been a part of. The male romance involves dreaming of the past in order to imagine our way into the future: if I could look long enough at my father's brothers I might pick up the secret of my belonging.

I am reminded of another photograph, a self-portrait by the Dutch photographer Hans van Manen. He has named it after Michelangelo's *Madonna and Christ* in St Peter's, Rome – *Pietà: Self-portrait with Thijs Westerbeek*. Michelangelo's sculpture depicts a sensuous, vulnerable body of the adult Christ lying in his mother's arms – a man must be dead or dying before he is portrayed in this state of blissful abandonment. And she, the icon of European motherhood, gazes down at her son with a mixture of resignation and desire. She has given her life to her son, and now she must lose him. In contrast, van Manen's self-portrait is an agony of discomfort. He sits, dressed in a pin-stripe suit and tie, hair neatly parted, brogues on his feet, with the sprawling body of a naked young man balanced precariously in his arms. He stares at the camera with a mixture of doubt and horror. Does he love the young man as a father, or does he love him sexually, or both? Is the naked young man an aspect of himself, a representation of his own body and sexuality, or a prefiguration of his own death? The picture offers only doubt and uncertainty. This is my body, his self-portrait proclaims, and I do not know what to do with it, I do not know what to say. His profound unease begs the question: What have men to say about themselves?

II

I look at myself in the small, chipped mirror I have placed on the bookshelf above my desk. I look at myself looking. I have an idea that I might see inside myself and begin to answer this question. I see my eyes, nose, mouth, forty-one years old. I look at my eyes and they reflect back to me nothing but my own looking. I look because I am trying to do more than look at myself. As with the photograph of my uncles, I want to describe what I am looking for. One of the great pleasures of adolescent hero-worship is its naiveté, its intense excitement and pleasure in life's possibilities. With maturity and a sceptical frame of mind we are frequently left floundering when we try to recapture that uncompromising belief in ourselves. We become aware of our incompleteness and the male romance loses some of its appeal. When I was a small boy I had a daydream about being famous. Wherever I walked people would turn and point and remark: 'That's J, the famous . . .' I basked in the promise of this recognition. I dreamed my life would be a train of events, each of which would touch me with my own humanity. Life would be a mirror, reflecting all my hopes and aspirations. Love would be my ultimate connection with this moment and with myself. Now when I look in the mirror I am looking for my relationships with others, something other than Narcissus' self-absorption.

When I was ten, there was a boy called C who sat at the back of the class and never spoke to anyone. He had short cropped hair and buck teeth, a pudgy face and an ungainly body. At break-time he would wander alone aimlessly, carefully circumventing our boisterous play as if he were fragile and contact with other boys would damage him. I felt pity for him and one break-time I walked up to him and said, 'C, do you want to play with me?' He gave me a curious stare and said no. He walked off, jumping aside as two boys hurtled towards him with a football. After that incident I no longer felt concern for him, not because I was aggrieved at his rejection, but because I knew he did not need me. I spent a number of years of my boyhood in a boarding school. The ages of the boys ranged from eight to twelve. Certainly we could be cruel to one another, but we also had sympathy. We defended ourselves from the masters' petty tyranny, offered rudimentary solace to boys who were homesick, and played together. We built camps and recreated our homes with piles of rotting leaves and the discarded limbs and roots of trees that had been torn down to make way for the playground. We replaced our families with gangs. It was a form of boy culture popularized by William Golding in his novel *Lord of the Flies*. A group of English, prep school boys are stranded on an island. Their attempts to organize themselves into a civilized and democratic body fail and they descend into barbarism and murder. Golding's pessimistic view of the psychology of boyhood has been used to justify the notion that boys, left to their own devices, are incapable of ethical behaviour and of caring for one another. This wasn't my experience when I was growing up. Golding, however, was writing an allegory about original sin. There is a contrasting story to tell about boys' relationships with each other which is closer to my own experience and more instructive about the way in which modern masculinity has been formed.

It begins with *Tom Brown's Schooldays*, written by Thomas Hughes and published in 1857. On a first reading, Hughes appears to celebrate the tough, physical, anti-intellectual masculinity which came to dominate English culture and its empire. Within a matter of hours of arriving at Rugby School as a new boy, Tom gallantly saves the day for School House in their football match against the rest of the school. Tom and his companion East become young heroes. But for Hughes a man's character lay in his domesticity and love of his family, not in individual feats of prowess and daring. The boys' fighting, their insubordination, their cribbing and poaching become a cause for concern to the headmaster. He asks a young master – a disguised portrait of the author – how the two boys could be made more dutiful. The young master replies: 'I think if either of them had some little boy to take care of, it would steady them.' Tom is made mentor to George Arthur, a pious, gentle new boy who suffers from poor health. Despite his physical frailty, Arthur exhibits a moral and spiritual courage from which Tom learns a new respect for himself. He develops an almost motherly, protective concern for Arthur: 'From morning till night he had the feeling of responsibility on his mind, and even if he left Arthur in their study or in the close for an hour, was never at ease till he had him in sight again.' When Arthur is ill with fever and close to death, Tom watches him as he sleeps on a sofa: 'the Western sun stole gently, lighting up his white face and golden hair. Tom remembered a German picture of an angel.'

There is an ambiguous quality to Hughes' prescriptive ideal of manliness because it does not exclude the 'feminine' traits of concern and feeling. The cultivation of male emotional friendships or 'manly love' by Hughes and others found an echo in Victorian literature, particularly poetry. However, in the last decade of the nineteenth century compassion and love in boyhood friendships were ousted by the imperial values of 'manliness, steadfastness and courage', which denigrated 'namby pamby' behaviour. The trial of Oscar Wilde in 1895 brought to an end any approval of passionate male friendships. The stiff upper lip and a sound, manly character asserted itself in public life. Feminine traits in a man became a sign of a deviant personality, or a 'snob-queer', as the Marquess of Queensberry described him. By the end of the century men's friendships were no longer free of suspicion, a phobic anxiety which created a boundary between sexual and non-sexual male relationships. Despite this, the ideals of manly love were revived during the First World War and continued to be celebrated. Countless public school stories promoted love and loyalty between boys as they walked arm in arm down the Close, chaste and inseparable. Horace Vachell's popular story *The Hill: A Romance of Friendship*, published in 1905, is an account of John (Jonathan) Verney's love for Desmond (Caeser). Romantic and sentimental, it is an unconscious eulogy of homosexual love.

'You like me, old Jonathan, don't you?'

'Awfully,' said John.

'Why did you look at me when you sang that last verse? Did you know that you were looking at me?'

'Yes.'

'You looked at me because – well because – bar chaff – you – liked – me?'

'Yes.'

'You like me better than any other fellow in the school?'

'Yes; better than any other fellow in the world.'

'Is it possible?'

'I have always felt that way ever since – yes – since the first moment I saw you . . . You smiled at me, Caeser. It warmed me through and through. I suppose when a fellow is starving he never forgets the first meal after it.'

At the heart of late-Victorian manliness lay an infatuation with boys' and men's boyishness, which was sublimated into these male romances. This yearning to return to boyhood carried with it that powerful emblem of upper-class English masculinity, the death wish, exemplified in Peter Pan's comment that 'to die would be an awfully big adventure'. Love between men had to be separated from the body and sex and so had to transcend both. Its ultimate and most noble expression was in death and self-sacrifice. At the end of *The Hill* Desmond dies in the Boer War. Verney is consoled by a final letter from his friend which tells him he is 'the only one I love as much as my own brother – *and even more*'. The proclamation of homoerotic love could find an outlet only in death: 'To die young, clean and ardent; to die swiftly, in perfect health; to die saving others from death, or worse – disgrace; to die scaling heights; to die and to carry with you into the fuller ampler life beyond, untainted hopes and aspirations, unembittered memories, all the freshness and gladness of May – is not that cause for joy rather than sorrow.'

The male romance continues to be a part of masculinity and culture. Vachell's *The Hill* is different in time and place from Rob Reiner's 1986 film *Stand By Me*, but they both evoke the same sentimental nostalgia for boyhood. *Stand By Me*, set in 1950s, small-town America, and based on a short story by Stephen King, is about four twelve-year-old boys, Geordie, Chris, Teddy and Vern, who go off on a hike in search of the body of a boy killed in a train accident. Each of their lives is blighted by poverty, authoritarian fathers and other problem adults. The summer is drawing to an

128

end and they are all due to begin new schools in the fall. There is a sense that the dead boy they seek represents the demise of their own childhoods.

The story, narrated by the grown-up Geordie, is a requiem for a lost age of boyish innocence, before hetero-sexuality suppresses boys' feelings for one another. Adolescence is depicted in the brutalized and cowardly bragging of a gang of older boys, whose threats of violence hover constantly in the background. Their competitive and unfeeling bravado is shown in marked contrast to the empathy of the younger boys. Puberty is portrayed as a kind of fall from grace after which love and affection between boys is replaced by fear and humiliation. The four friends follow the railway track into the country and, after two days' walking, they discover the body hidden by bushes at the bottom of the railway bank. It's as if claiming the dead boy as their own, releases them from a state of mourning, helping them to come to terms with a passing phase of their lives. In the final sequence of the film the middle-aged Geordie describes the fate of his three friends. Vern and Teddy lead unhappy lives and Chris was killed as a young adult intervening in a bar-room fight. The camera focuses on Geordie's computer screen as he types the final lines of the script, reflecting on the intensity and transience of boyhood friendships. 'I never had any friends later on like the ones I had when I was twelve. Jesus, does anyone?'

Men look upon their boyhoods as a distinct and special period of their lives: after puberty nothing is the same again. Adolescence is a transition out of the past; it is a period of bereavement. I can remember a similar summer when I was fifteen and felt that my own boyhood had come to an end. My family was spending August by the sea, in the place we had stayed for over ten years. It wasn't our last family holiday; that was the following year. I remember these holidays as the most untrammelled weeks of my childhood. This particular year a new disco had opened in a nearby hotel. R, a close friend who was a year older than me, insisted we go. I arrived at the disco nervous, reticent and half dressed up, expecting to be denied entrance. We paid and walked past the doorman into the sound of Hawkwind's 'Silver Machine'. At such moments it is possible to feel a simultaneous exhilaration and dread, as if something is beginning and ending in the same instant. During our holidays R and I had been inseparable, messing about together, swimming, sailing and rowing in his small dinghy. After the disco opened all this seemed to change. Our evenings were spent gazing across the strobed dance floor working up the courage to ask a girl to dance, whispering messages that X fancied Y and chatting up girls. The following day we detailed the failures and successes of the previous night. One afternoon R and I were swimming in the sea and I climbed onto a raft anchored off the beach as a resting-place for swimmers. R remained in the water, his arms folded along the edge of the raft. I was wearing a turquoise T-shirt which laced up at the neck and of which I was particularly proud. R nodded at my T-shirt and told me that turquoise was the colour worn by French queers. I was embarrassed and said I hadn't realized this and mumbled some excuse for wearing it. When we had recovered our breath we swam back to the shore and parted company until our evening rendezvous at the disco. Sexuality had come into our lives and so had a new wariness about our relationship with each other. As I walked back along the beach I took off my T-shirt and pushed it into a waste bin. I told my mother I had lost it.

The insouciance of boyhood disappears in the anxiety to create an acceptable masquerade of masculinity: to learn how to walk down the street, how to hold one's body around other boys, how to touch other boys in ways that are not suggestive of intimacy; how to disguise fear, doubt, uncertainty, unease and to feign indifference to aggression, humiliation and acts of petty violence; how to discuss girls and women without hinting at feelings of need and in a way that enhances personal sexual prestige. To create a façade of assured self-confidence – to be complete in oneself, fully present and unfazed by the world around you. I could never manage this with any noticeable degree of competence – what boy can? – but it did not stop me trying to measure up to the masquerade. At the back of one's mind was the fear of being exposed as a pouf, queer, bender, sissy, woman. And always the possibility of shame, humiliation and violence. Sexual insecurity is endogenous to masculinity. If society has manufactured such loathing for homosexuality that young men are made to feel anxious about their own feelings and their sexual uncertainty, then some will attempt to kick, punch, stab and humiliate their way into saving face. The paper *Capital Gay* reported one incident: 'These four lads came toward us and shouted "Queers." Then all hell broke loose. I was punched and kicked to the ground . . . Suddenly there was a shout and they all ran off. I got up and saw Richard lying in a pool of blood. His left eye had been split open. Somebody lifted his shirt and there was blood pumping out of the side of his body.' In this masculine world heterosexuality must constantly be proven to other boys and men.

I recall an incident that took place shortly after I had returned from our family holiday. I was out walking with a friend down a long, straight road. It was late on a Sunday afternoon, towards the end of September. Either side of us were fallow fields hedged by woods. There were few cars and it was very peaceful. As we walked a car drove up fast and slewed towards us. Four men were crammed inside, one of whom stuck his head out of the window and screamed abuse at us. His long hair straggled across his pasty, white face. A, beside me, stuck two fingers in the air in a gesture of defiance. Two hundred metres ahead the car stopped suddenly and remained stationary. We stopped. There was no one about and nowhere to run to.

The car began reversing, back towards us. Its engine whined as cars do when they're reversing too fast. It stopped beside A. The man in the passenger seat with the straggly hair said: 'What are you up to, you little cunt?' A told him: 'Fuck off.' Two of the men clambered out of the car and attacked A. They weren't boys; these were young men, befuddled by Sunday drinking. They punched and kicked, their faces alive with contempt and hatred. I wanted to hate them back for their ungainly punches and brutish, stupid expressions and for my own impotence. I wanted to defend myself with the same vehemence, but I was numbed by fear. And A was shouting at them 'Bugger off, bugger off' as if, unlike me, he would rather die than submit to them. Winded and breathing heavily, they turned on me and told me to keep my mouth shut. 'Yes,' I said. My words were strangled and felt hoarse and high and half-dead. I was too afraid to be ashamed.

'What did you say, cunt?'

'Yes. I said I will, yes.'

'You bastards!' A began to shout.

I turned on him. He was clutching his stomach, doubled over. 'Don't, A. Don't. Be quiet. Let them go.' The biggest of the two men – he had sandy hair and a face that was too red – turned round and punched me. I felt nothing, simply landed on my back on the roadside and sat up. Then they climbed into the car and drove off. We didn't tell anybody. They caught up with us a mile down the road, two car loads of them, and issued several more threats and punches to ensure our silence. For a year afterwards I never went into the nearby town. I had collaborated in my own humiliation and felt a coward. Young men constituted a potential threat and I adapted accordingly.

We live in and are formed by a web and history of relationships. Our genes give us predispositions, our parents influence our personalities, but it is the language we grow up with that gives meaning to ourselves. The male romance is part of a culture still dominated by men's voices and unspoken feelings. It is the expression of our narcissistic love of self and other men, a defensive, embattled form of love threatened by its own sometimes violent contradictions. Women don't appear to be a part of this emotional life of masculinity, and yet they are never absent. If I look up and catch sight of the mirror I placed on my bookshelf, I can see a photograph of my mother which hangs on the wall behind me. She is looking directly into the camera and so at me. Women are not the objects of the male romance, but they define the relationships between men. Shane rode away from the Starrett homestead because he was in love with Joey's mother. Ethan Edwards turned his back on the doorway of the Jorgensens' homestead because a domestic life loving a woman frightened him more than the desert and the Indians. Between men there are women. Women occupy a position in society which literally and symbolically governs men's relationships with one another. The French anthropologist Claude Lévi-Strauss argues that society is made up of relationships between men which are determined by the exchange of women. Marriage, for example, is not simply a relationship between a man and a woman, but between two groups of men. The woman is the object in the exchange, not one of the partners. In *The Searchers* the renegade Scar and his pursuer Ethan Edwards fight over Debbie. In *Shane* Joe Starrett and Shane are in competition for Marion. Lévi-Strauss argues that women are used by men as 'a conduit for a relationship' with other men. Gender is a triangular relationship. Men have competed for women, who have been used as an object in the transactions of property, business and inheritance. They have been used to confirm a man's heterosexuality, to legitimize his claim to his masculine status and to enable him to win standing amongst other men.

A graphic illustration of this triangular relationship is Brian de Palma's Vietnam film *Casualties of War*. A group of GIs kidnap a young Vietnamese woman with the intention of raping her. They take her out on patrol and come across a deserted hamlet; this, according to their sergeant, Meserve, is a suitable place. The story is an example of how the male romance can turn savage. It shows how the men's relationships with one another are defined by their relationship with the women they have kidnapped. One of the soldiers, Private Eriksson, refuses to participate in the rape. He demands that the woman is released unharmed. His refusal to collude in the act provokes a crisis amongst the men. Integral to the rape must be the culpability of the whole group. Private Diaz, a teenage boy, pleads secretly with Eriksson to help him avoid having to rape the woman. Meserve, backed up by the other men, attempts to enforce conformity within the group by accusing waverers of homosexuality. Eriksson is taunted and ridiculed for being a faggot. 'Stop looking at Diaz,' yells Meserve. 'Maybe Diaz is homosexual. We've got ourselves two girls in the patrol.' Meserve threatens Eriksson: 'Maybe when I'm done with her, I'm going to come after you.' The other men look on knowingly. Such an act will not undermine the masculine prowess of Meserve, but it will reduce Eriksson to the status of a woman. Eriksson refuses to be intimidated and is forcibly prevented from intervening. Diaz, terrified of exposing his vulnerability to the other men, rapes the woman. A number of critics of the film were angry at the way the woman was objectified as a silent, terrified and passive victim. They accused the film-maker of misogyny and racism, and of denying her a voice. But perhaps this is the point. In a society like our own, which still retains the language and culture of its patriarchal past, women are silenced and remain as the object of exchange between men, if no longer literally in the forging of family alliances, then symbolically and metaphorically. In *Casualties of War* the woman is a 'dink' who exists as an object of sexual pleasure which is exchanged amongst the men and used to confirm their place in the white American brotherhood. What makes this particular story possible is not the woman's protest – she has no voice in this male social order – but the refusal of one man to conform. Without his story there would be no story.

This is the dark and destructive side of the male romance – a society which privileges the male and fosters a dread of homosexuality and a hatred of women. Its corollary is men's violence against women. In extremis, it is the story of men like Peter Sutcliffe, the Yorkshire Ripper, who murdered thirteen women and left a further six grievously injured. In her book *The Street-Cleaner* Nicole Ward Jouve writes that Sutcliffe was a small, physically weak and shy boy who stuck close to his mother and enjoyed reading. He was unwilling to join in the boisterous play of other boys and disliked sports. He was seen as being 'deep'. In the working-class male culture he grew up in such behaviour was seen as 'girlish'. He started work at the age of sixteen, and was remembered by his colleagues as being a 'queer bugger', a 'frightened animal'. The industrial environment didn't suit him. Sutcliffe was shy with girls, but he had a close friend called Keith Sugden. Both were 'mother's boys'. Sutcliffe spent a great deal of time with Sugden, who used to be asked by other young men how his 'boyfriend' was. Keith's mother is reported to have said: 'There was a time when I used to think that Peter was in love with Keith.' When Sutcliffe was eighteen he made a concerted effort to adapt to the male world. He read the Charles Atlas magazine ads: 'One day, I discovered a secret that changed me from a timid, frightened 97 pound weakling into "The World's Most Perfectly Developed Man" . . . a real He-Man . . . a man who STANDS OUT in any crowd.' The comic strip accompanying the ad shows Mac becoming a Man. He knocks down the beach bully in front of his girlfriend, affirming his virility and proving himself to her. Again that triangular relationship. Sutcliffe began body-building.

Sutcliffe's acceptance into the masculine world was eased by banter and jokes. When he indulged in these he could feel that his mates were with him. On several occasions before he began killing he went out, armed with a sockful of gravel or a brick, to attack a woman while his friend Trevor Birdsall sat and waited for him in the car. The killing became possible because of men's cultural attitudes towards women and prostitutes. At one point Leeds football fans chanted 'Eleven—nil', meaning eleven known victims to the Ripper, no result for the police. Would they have chanted that for a child murderer? Prostitutes were fair game. Like many men, Sutcliffe wanted to shut women up, only he went way beyond society's normal means of excluding women from male domains through wife-beating and sexist put-downs. Women were his persecutors and God had called on him to cleanse from the streets the filth and pollution embodied by prostitutes. By ridding the world of 'bad' female sexual desire he could preserve his own narcissistic world. If women were silenced then he would be released from any obligation to them. He would be free to live out his life in the company of men. Killing women stimulated Sutcliffe's male romance.

III

A female friend read this chapter and wrote back and told me that ending on Sutcliffe seemed appropriate. I asked a male friend and he was uncomfortable with this ending. He said it tarred all men with the same brush and would put men off reading the book. It hinted at that old radical feminist argument that all men are potential rapists. His comments reminded me of the launch of a book on masculinity. A creative director from a leading advertising company stood up and agreed that the book addressed an important subject, but he felt that male readers would be frightened off by its anti-male tone. Self-analysis causes consternation and touches on a deeper level of self-dislike in men.

I met S when I was twenty-five. He was my age, a tall man who wore his hair long. He was never much of a dresser and his clothes were usually old and worn. I used to sit with him in his kitchen while our children played. He would make a pot of tea, sit down, cross his legs and roll a scrawny cigarette which he stuck in his mouth and lit with a match from a box of Swan Vestas. We lived some distance from one another and when we parted we would not see each other for several months. We kept in contact by letter and phone: it was always just enough to sustain our friendship. However, the distance between us remained undiminished over the years, as if we were travelling along parallel tracks.

The problem in S's life was his lack of self-esteem. He did not like himself as a man. He believed that men loved women out of self-interest rather than empathy. The male romance – men's narcissism – overwhelmed him with guilt. When he was in this frame of mind he would vacillate and sink into inertia and have few good words to say about himself or men in general. Ten years later S was seriously ill and dying. On one of the last occasions I saw him he was standing in his living room, staring out of the window. I hadn't seen him for six months and we cast around for threads from the past. Our conversation was desultory and I followed his gaze into the garden. When he moved into this large house the garden had been wild and overgrown. Now it was cultivated, the lawn was mown and the bramble thickets at the end near the stone wall had been cut down and burnt. The apple tree which had sprawled across the pathway, broken and surrounded by rotting fruit, had been pruned and tidied. Like a coppice, everything had been cut back to its beginnings. I thought I would break the silence and say something about this garden and how it had changed. I looked at S, his hair alight in the sun, his hands quite still, resting on the table. His thoughts were elsewhere and I didn't know what to say to him. Despite all the years we had known each other, when I looked at him I felt only the distance between us.

I attended S's funeral. After his cancer was diagnosed, he had acquired a new set of friends. They bore witness to his love and his sense of purpose in life. They were honoured to have known him. But he was both more and less than their eulogies and I did not recognize the man I had known in their descriptions. They had left something out.

Now van Manen's self-portrait makes sense to me. He lays bare – literally – men's unease with ourselves, our fear of each other, our own nakedness and vulnerability. We hide in our male romance, we use its illusions like a veil of silence that descends between us. In adulthood, when it is harder to dream about the future, we should cling not to the heroes of our adolescence, but to the way in which we made use of them, to the belief in ourselves they helped to instil. S had lacked this verve until, confronted by death, he found it. Freud wrote that a man will choose to love what he himself is, what he himself was, or what he himself would like to be, and someone who was once a part of himself. In our love of women, a part of us seeks to recover our attachment to our mothers. In the men we love we seek the father we once idealized. In each case we love what has been lost to us. There is nothing to be gained in guilt, only in acknowledging that to love ourselves we must love and be loved by another, and to love another we must be able to love ourselves. And last: men may struggle to love themselves and other men, be willing and able to love their mothers and fathers and children, but loving women is the hardest thing to do.

6

SEDUCTION

It is love. I will have to flee or hide.

JORGE LUIS BORGES

I

I once attended a seminar where a man was trying to convey his thoughts on compassion. He was making a point about how we might learn to empathize with others. He finished with a poem, 'Love's Philosophy' by Percy Bysshe Shelley, and recited the final verse:

> See the mountains kiss high Heaven
>   And the waves clasp one another;
> No sister flower would be forgiven
>   If it disdained its brother;
> And the sunlight clasps the earth
>   And the moonbeams kiss the sea;
> What is all this sweet work worth
>   If thou love not me?

141

Several days after the meeting I found a book by Shelley, and read 'Love's Philosophy'. I discovered that the speaker had changed the last line. Shelley had written: 'What is all this sweet work worth / If thou kiss not me?' He had substituted the word 'love' for 'kiss'. One word, and yet the meaning of the poem was dramatically changed. It is not a poem of love, it is a poem of seduction, written to Sophie Stacey, a young cousin who attracted Shelley.

The most celebrated legend of masculine sexuality is the myth of the libertine Don Juan. Originating in Tirso de Molina's story *El Burlador de Sevilla* in 1630, he entered the European imagination with the production of Mozart's *Don Giovanni* in Prague in 1787. Don Giovanni boasts to his servant Leporello, 'I can make love to whom I please! / Ah, by tomorrow morning, my list should have grown by a dozen or so.' He seduces women like he drinks wine, simply because he can. His toast is to freedom. Challenged by Leporello to mend his ways and to leave women alone, Don Giovanni is shocked by the idea that he is doing wrong:

> It's all part of love.
> If a man keeps faith with one,
> he is cruel to all the others;
> I, who know myself to be
> a man of boundless generosity,
> love them each and every one.

He loves the idea of women, but not one woman in particular. He is a man without relationships, a narcissist governed by his own gratification. The freedom he celebrates is his licence to escape commitment. He seduces women endlessly,

not because he is chasing an ideal but because he is compelled to deny his own need. He is a ladies' man. He loves
the quarry, the chase, the bed, the sex. The appeal of
seduction lies in his separation of desire from need: the
illusion of pure sex, unencumbered by intimacy or commitment. Proust and Stendhal wrote in order to alleviate their
lovelessness, to discover how to be alone with themselves.
Don Juan fucks in order to escape such contemplation. He
is a man who cannot be still. He imagines that if he stays
with one woman she will hold him captive and he will feel
as if his life is expiring. He cannot be without women, and
yet he cannot abide to live with them. It is the pursuit
which provides him with a sense of being alive; he hopes
that the next sexual conquest will fulfil him and banish his
feeling of emptiness. It never does. Satisfied, satiated, there
is nothing left but disappointment and the exhausting
knowledge that it must be done all over again.

Every man has grown up in a culture in which sex, his
own sexuality, his self are defined and judged by the practice
of seduction. In our teenage years we learn that to tempt
or entice sex from girls is a sign that we now belong to the
fraternity of men. Open any teen romance magazine today
and the principal characters will be girls. Girls learn the
language of emotions, love and romance from an early age.
They concern themselves with the problems and predica-
ments of their relationships. For boys, love and relationships
with girls are expressed through the language of having sex.
Boys in romance comics talk like 'Damon' in *My Guy*: '. . . so
when she said "come up to my room" I thought "ha-way
the lads – we're on." ' Male desire is about doing, acting

on others, imposing, thrusting, pushing and achieving. It's not just the technique; it becomes a state of being, a regime of pursuit and capture and the need to be acknowledged as a man by other men. Above all, male desire is repetitious. When we desire a woman we imagine nothing will ever be the same again, and yet everything always remains the same.

I've been thinking about confession – not the religious confession of sin, but of sex. Sex involves confessing. We live in a culture which attempts to tame desire by confessing it; owning up to our sexual desires has become a secular act of penitence and moral self-improvement. Michel Foucault's argument that we use sex to define 'the truth of ourselves' appears to be proven by its sheer omnipresence and babble: the self-help manuals, the tabloid exposures and relentless pursuit of sexual travesties, the counselling, the agony columns, the advice lines ('How Men Can Make Love Longer', 'Your Man Gone Off the Boil?', 'Women and Orgasm'); the books and videos promising to improve your sexual technique (*The Essential Lover's Guide* video assures the viewer it will 'open up the subject in an appealing and sensitive way . . . Never before has sex and love been portrayed so openly and honestly'); the writers and journalists talking about their sexual preferences, divorces and marital infidelities. Sex is loudly and endlessly exhibited and yet this noisiest of preoccupations tells us relatively little about our bodies and pleasure. We are bombarded with tantalizing images of what we imagine other people do, but rarely do ourselves. Since the 1960s the aura of sex has become tarnished.

Sex is a fiction. We search exhaustively to discover its secret meaning – the essence of our being – but there are no secret meanings. As we talk about sex we invent its meanings. In male company, men will talk about sex and women because if they talk for long enough they may convince themselves and other men that they belong to the fraternity. Talking about sex reflects men's obsessive need to belong, to get things straight and know where they stand; 'to know what I've got and what she hasn't'; to invent an imagined unity among themselves. On the cover of men's magazines scantily clad women tempt, beckon and simper because, in a masculine culture which highlights personal insecurity, young men need that kind of reassurance. The late Michael Vermeulan, outraged that *GQ*, his up-market magazine for thirty-something men, might be thought less laddish than *Loaded*, declared: 'We had a headline that said "How to Pull the Chicks, Sex, Sex, Sex" years ago . . . There is no such thing as New Man. That stuff is bullshit.' The louder the clamour the greater the pathos. Men together do not talk about pleasure or speak about their bodies; they confess the numbers of women, the places, times and sexual positions. Men use sex to master women but, paradoxically, it threatens to master them. Initiation into sex is the votive force of masculinity, the emblem of male virility and it is fraught with the possibilities of failure and humiliation.

Today I phoned a friend. She asked me how my writing was going and I told her I was stonewalled. She asked me why and I explained that I was trying to write about sex. 'Explained', however, is not the right word because I couldn't explain to her what was obstructing me. I said to her: 'I don't want to confess to anything. But if I don't I will have nothing to say.' She agreed this was a problem

and we talked about other things. Eventually, because it
was playing on my mind, I returned to the subject. I mentioned to her the trial at the Old Bailey of four boys, three
aged ten and one aged eleven, who had been accused of the
rape and indecent assault of a young girl. The boys were
alleged to have pushed her into the boys' toilets in the lunch
break, stripped her and thrown her coat over her head. Three
of them were accused of penetrating her. In her testimony
to the court the young girl reported that one boy had refused
to join in with the other boys. 'They were telling him to
come and he was saying, "I ain't going to come" . . . I said,
"Please don't hurt me," and he said, "I am not going to
hurt you because you are my friend." ' She added: 'They
were telling him and they were cursing him because he said
no. They wanted him to lie on top of me.' The boys were
acquitted, but I mentioned to my friend how the young
girl's description of events was a replica of de Palma's film
Casualties of War. Was there something innately violent and
intractable about male sexual desire? My friend had no
answer to this, but she replied: 'That's the story to follow,
the story of the girl and the boy who refused.' Is this my
story also? Or do I belong with the other three boys? Like
most men I have been a part of both.

II

On my first day at prep school I sat next to a boy called B
in assembly. The numbers of the hymns we would sing that
morning were displayed on a small rack on the wall of the

school hall. As the headmaster stood up to speak, I began to argue with B about which hymn number we should turn to in our hymn books. We had each turned to different numbers and were both emphatic that ours was the correct one. When the rest of the school began singing we were both proved right. B was a Catholic and had a hymn book with different hymn numbers to my own Anglican version. After that inauspicious start we became best friends, a relationship which lasted until we were seventeen, when we grew apart. At thirteen, we shared the experience of our first girlfriends. Unlike me, B was an incorrigible socialite who took great pleasure in the complex and often tortuous intricacies of our burgeoning teenage affairs. The first object of his desire – she could not have been described as his girlfriend – lived in a bungalow which backed onto a public footpath. Every evening B would insist we walk down this path and peer in through the broken garden fence. On our hands and knees we could see a compost heap and, by turning our heads, a path leading up to a set of French windows. By climbing onto my shoulders, B could look over the fence to the attic window, which he believed was the bedroom of his beloved. It left him exposed to the watchful eye of the girl's father, and so he was unwilling to risk this clear view unless he was sure of sighting her. I don't recall that we ever saw her. I don't believe that B ever talked to this girl more than twice. But an image of her occupied his waking hours; she was a perennial topic of his conversation and he would eagerly recount his fleeting glances of her, as she climbed onto the motorbikes of her older and more sophisticated boyfriends.

Perhaps B was attracted to unrequited love, for he invariably set his sights on girls who were beyond the reach of a podgy thirteen-year-old. He invested girls with magic and he would urge me to join him in his intoxication. My mother, much to my annoyance, had signed me up for dancing lessons at the local Masonic Hall. In spite of my lack of enthusiasm, B urged me to attend, for here I would be able to meet girls. And it was here that I met K. The Masonic Hall was a neglected-looking building at the far end of our local row of shops. Occasionally when I was young and we were visiting the newsagents to buy our Saturday morning sweets and there was nowhere along the roadside to park, my father would park in its small rear car park; it was a round-the-back, out-of-the-way place, which lent the hall an element of mystery. And it was here each Monday night for six weeks that Mrs R, a woman with a sense of humour and a warm Scottish burr, would arrive with her portable record player. We children, or young teenagers as we were by then, would sit on chairs placed around the edge of the hall, alone or in pairs, waiting for Mrs R's instructions. The bare hall had the musty smell of a forsaken world. I think this is how we always met girls in my young teens, fixed around the edge of rooms and dance halls, surreptitiously eyeing each other up, immobilized by our nervousness. The atmosphere was soon enlivened by Mrs R's selection of dated 45s. 'OK, let's begin with this one', she would say, as she wrestled with the old three-pin plug, and slipped a stack of discs onto the record player. The soft clunk of the first dropping down onto the rubber of the turntable signalled our drift onto the floor and the scratchy sound of her opener: 'Woke up this morning feeling fine, there's something special on my mind.'

I noticed K on the first night. She had long brown hair and large front teeth. She had a nervous smile she was quick to share with everyone. And yet she was self-possessed. I wanted to be her partner. Each lesson became infused with my longing to embrace her slight, skinny body as we shuffled our way through the waltz, or to hold her hand as we manoeuvred through one of Mrs R's Scottish dances. I liked K. We talked together. But more than that I wanted her. I wanted to inhale her smell and touch her. We arranged to meet in a local park and went walking together in a chaste and awkward perambulation across the grass and around the pond, and at a loss to know what to do with each other – although I knew I wanted to lie down by that tree and kiss her, but was too shy, too fearful of rejection, to propose this. During term time we wrote to one another and I still have one of her letters, written on purple paper, detailing the convoluted affairs of our mutual acquaintances: 'I have written to Dave twice, actually he wrote me another letter. Why did Claire go off with Dave? Didn't he like Marie anymore? I think that's really sad. I bet Marie's upset, oh well it's his affair.'

When I finally kissed K my heart was already set on another girl. I never said goodbye to her, but pursued my new infatuation. I didn't know this girl well. I had noticed her at a local dance. She was the daughter of a doctor and I thought she was beautiful. I managed to put my arms around her and kiss her and feel her small breasts, but she remained aloof and let me know in numerous impalpable ways that I was too juvenile for her. Impalpable, I say, but as B pointed out to me, when she went out with a boy who owned a car and my brief passion came to nothing, my love was blind. It was a cliché that applied to B, who was besotted with a beautiful girl sought after by every boy in the area. He was a hopeless outsider alongside her never-ending queue of suave, well-dressed and handsome suitors. But he showed a fidelity to her the others lacked, and with his dogged determination, he was willing for a long haul. In the end he never did win her love. Years later he had a relationship with her younger sister, an affair which failed to deliver the promise of his unrequited love.

There was something harmless about our early infatuations which changed as we got older. For B it was his doomed and misplaced fidelity. For myself it was that summer holiday when the disco and sex became part of my life. It had been there before, but it had lacked the quality of a competitive, face-saving performance. It was much the same as team games at school. The junior sides knocked each other about, but for the sixteen-year-olds, team games took a noticeable turn to aggression and violence. So it was with sex: the game was the same, only now there was a lot more at stake. One Sunday morning I was walking down the high street when I was approached by a girl my own age. She looked at me with a degree of familiarity and smiled and said hello. I felt awkward. We talked briefly and then she said she had to walk up to the supermarket as her mother wanted some milk. She was hoping that I would accompany her. Instead I said goodbye. I had met her a few days before at the disco. Even now I remember sitting on the beach with her, our mouths sore with kissing, my insistent hands searching over her body, disappointed by her resistance. What had possessed me to be so insensitive?

Kissing and leaving was the story of my boyhood sexual adventures. As I got older I began to feel self-conscious and insecure about my sexuality and relationships – feelings which I attempted to manage by keeping out of people's way. Because I had always looked younger than my age, I was frequently accused of being homosexual or challenged to prove my sexual experience. By the time I was eighteen the issue of sex had become fraught. One lunchtime I was walking to a local pub with my English teacher and a group of students from my sixth form college. I was wearing a new jacket that was an unconventional yellow. One of the older students, a man who exuded self-assurance, butted in to my conversation, gripped hold of my jacket and asked me if I was a fag. I denied that I was. 'I bet he's never slept with a woman,' he said to the other students and turned to look at me, waiting for my reply. I said nothing because I hadn't, and felt that this was a terrible humiliation. I had neither the wit nor the self-confidence to defend myself against his sexual taunts, and was only saved from further ignominy by the intervention of my teacher. Later she told me to take no notice. But I did take notice. I paid careful attention to conversations I was involved in, wary of being drawn into other young men's sexual banter. Somehow, I wasn't a man. Not just 'not a man', I couldn't become myself. I felt myself exposed for other men to wipe their feet on. It didn't matter that the majority of other young men lied about their sexual experience and that those who bragged about fucking also lied, or practised a crude, perfunctory sexual intercourse. The majority of young men, sexually inexperienced, uninterested, gay or wary of the advances of young women, practised the wily art of evading the topic of sex. They conformed to the dominant myths about male heterosexuality because they dreaded being exposed. In this masculine culture, virginity was a source of almost unendurable shame.

The weekend following this incident there was a college disco. Y, a young woman I had known for years, had been invited. Y had sex with boys because she needed to feel loved. She knew this and it created terrible problems for her, because boys couldn't give her what she needed. All they gave her was a reputation for being 'easy'. That night I was talking to her on the stairs. I can't remember what we were talking about, though we used to have long conversations. Two young men walked up the stairs towards us. I knew them and didn't like them. We'd known each other since childhood. In our early teens they'd been skinheads and had enjoyed getting into drunken fights. They graduated into a local bikers' group and wore the colours of a chapter of the Hell's Angels. They weren't Hell's Angels, they were fakes. Nevertheless they gave off a frisson of violence which made me wary of them. As they walked up the stairs they were dressed in casuals, junior managers in a local mental hospital now, but still emanating an overweening arrogance. As they passed us they nudged Y and guided her up the stairs. They were pleased to see me and asked me how I was, as if Y, who was now standing between them, didn't exist. As I stood and watched and she protested mildly – she knew them, she'd had sex with them both, she expected this – they took her into a room. At the time I didn't think, they're raping her! After all, she went with them. She walked into the room of her own volition. But that's what they did: they wanted her and so they took her and fucked her, and if she'd denied them, or resisted, they would have been aggressive, they might have been violent, they would have persisted or forced her.

III

Reach for the top shelf. Stretch up, up past the motoring magazines, the angling and motor sport to the dwindling row of titles cramped on the end. Take it nonchalantly to the counter and pay your money and slip it into your bag. Porn. Women. 'I'm not kidding you, I'm not joking, that's what they did. They shared my spunk out that way. Delia licked it all, every last drop, from Sue's face, and this gave them both climaxes.' Len is a waiter, describing his sexual exploits in a soft porn magazine. He has discovered two women in a hotel bedroom 'in the sixty-nine position and sucking each other out'. They invite him to join them. 'Now it has always been my dream to be sucked off by two women at the same time.' But Len's fantasy-come-true seems to hold little pleasure for him. In his story the women moan, groan, pant and cry out in ecstasy. Len pumps and grinds and performs without any apparent loss of control. He isn't so much enjoying himself as trying to prove something. To consume pornography is to be the eternal seducer who wields a sexual mastery over female bodies. Pornography enables men to evade their dependency on women. Here, unlike in the real world, women are willing to be the objects of desire rather than the subjects of love.

Pornographic fantasy is male desire parodied by the bodies and actions of women. Just as women in relationships will give words to men's own unspoken feelings, so in pornography it is women who fabricate an image of a man's sexual allure. Len is not particularly interested in the women; he is performing for an imaginary audience of other men. He wants them to watch his performance, and take his place in their imaginations. The women's apparent compliance proves his manhood to them, proves that he is untainted by homosexuality. And yet there is an ambiguous quality to his concern about other men. A majority of the correspondence in the *Fiesta Reader's Letters Book* describes men who are turned on by sharing their wives with other men. 'Mick of Surrey' meets a man called Carl outside the school where his wife Kate works as a PE teacher. Together they admire Kate as she bends over to pick up a netball. 'It was really erotic hearing him praising her lovely figure and telling me how he would love to screw the ass off her.' Mick, Kate and Carl go for a meal in a quiet pub on the outskirts of the village where they live. One things leads to another: 'My mind was reeling as I watched this complete stranger fucking my wife.' In another letter 'Jack of Essex' watches as 'My horny slut of a wife had a stiff cock in each hand, tossing off Pete with one hand and taking Roy into her mouth with the other, her tits were being manhandled and sucked, and her legs were splayed apart, arse and cunt open and ready. She was begging to be fucked. And two more throbbing cocks were ready to do it.' 'John of Bolton' watches Roy 'thrust his fat cock deep inside' his wife and then 'Mike took his place between my lovely wife's thighs.' 'Danny of Southampton' is greeted by the sight of his wife Elaine's 'cunt filled to the brim with Dick's huge cock'. This image of male heterosexual desire is a monotonous reel of passive men aroused by strange men fucking their excited, willing wives – 'it was out of this world having two pricks fucking my cunt.' The characters in these male fantasies are interchangeable, but the scene remains unchanged – men exchange a woman and forge a bond between themselves.

'James of Coventry' describes his wife Claire as 'a little slut'. He is aroused by her ability to attract other men. He is proud of the way she brings them home for sex. He lies in their bed at night listening to her fucking strange men in the spare room. He plans the 'ultimate birthday present' for her. After a night out clubbing they arrive home to find six of her former lovers waiting for them. James has found their phone numbers from his wife's little black book and invited them over. Soon she is 'tumbling playfully' into the arms of Rick. 'Claire fucked him for a couple of minutes just like that. Every man in the room was working himself to a frenzy.' Next in line is Barry, 'bollock naked'. After him, Claire the 'self respecting cock sucker' sucks off Bob and Phil – 'Sticky spunk seemed to be squirting into her hungrily gulping throat and spattering against her face.' James details the exhaustive sexual performance of his wife that night – Clare 'fucked, sucked and swallowed'. By 3.30 a.m. Clare was on her knees again, at last swallowing my pent up jism while Rick took her from behind and Ian filmed proceedings with his camcorder.' It's the fantasy of a gang rape in which the men are goaded on by the woman: 'Wanking and sucking each cock in turn, she performed like some slut in the seediest of adult movies leaving a definite air of stunned disbelief hanging in the air like a smokescreen.' This disbelief, the extraordinary spectacle of seven men having sex with one woman, is all her doing. The idealized, chaste wife has been transformed into a whore who has possessed them. The men can surrender responsibility for their own actions. Their desire is no longer their own. Pornography acts like a smokescreen, obscuring men's actual lives and emotions; like an anaesthetic it dulls their doubts about the consequences of their sexual desire. They can fuck whoever and whatever they want.

In October 1997 a young woman, described in the press as a 'barmaid', testified in court to her alleged rape by six young army officers. The men had pulled off her clothes.

I felt frightened. I had already tried to get them off me, but they weren't listening to me. Phil went across to the TV and put on a pornographic video and I said it was disgusting. One of them said: 'Aren't you into group sex.' I was nervous because of the atmosphere and because of his question. I just wanted to get out. I was trying to put my jeans on and one of the lads came across to me and pushed me back onto the bed. I told him to get off, but he told me to lie there and enjoy it. A couple of them were in the corner on the far side of the room. Nick was to my left and Phil was to my right. They

156

were very close. They started playing with my breasts and [Darren] started having sex with me. Darren got off and Nick got on.

Another attempted to force her into oral sex. 'I think then Nick got off and Matt got on. I was very upset.' She said they were 'all laughing' – mainly at Phil, who was unable to perform. Two days later she received a bouquet with apologies for 'any misunderstanding'.

Men make a habit of sexually misunderstanding women. Male desire fragments and annuls a woman. It breaks up her wholeness and reduces her to a body of unconnected parts. The figure of the woman in pornography in the masculine imagination is the antithesis of the idealized figure of the mother. She is profane, alluring and sexually voracious. Unlike the figure of the mother, who threatens the male ego, she is 'dirtied' by her apparent moral degeneracy and so rendered safe and harmless. She is the 'slut' who embodies sex without the encumbrances of love and need. She becomes an object that can be used ruthlessly in the abandonment of sexual ecstasy and orgasm. In orgasm we momentarily lose ourselves. Something occurs and is destroyed and in this loss a substitute is created; desire is reborn. The pleasure of orgasm lies in the agony of this familiar death and renewal. Like a rollercoaster ride at a funfair, desire is the flirtation with our own violent death, knowing that we are secure from danger. Only men are never sure that we are secure from danger. The anxiety demands a speedy retreat back into ourselves. 'The demand for speed, for "quickness" turns me cold,' writes Phyllis Chessler. 'What demon do men run from . . . what enemy waits to envelop them from within, if they pause a bit in the taking – if not in the giving – of sexual pleasure?' One answer to her question can be found in the life of Jack Kerouac as he began his descent into personal dissolution. He wrote in *Big Sur*:

> But there's an awful paranoiac element sometimes in orgasm that suddenly releases not sweet genteel sympathy but some token venom that splits up the body – I feel a great ghastly hatred of myself and everything, the empty feeling far from being the usual relief is now as though I've been robbed of my spinal power right down the middle on purpose by a great witching force.

Orgasm confronts Kerouac, as it does Don Juan, with his own deadness. He returns into himself and the portcullis descends. He resides in his loneliness until, like an addict impelled to seek another fix, he is tempted out by the 'witching force' of his need for women.

Perhaps this is why, traditionally, pornography is consumed by men alone or men together: safety in numbers, safety in sameness. The woman in pornography is men's defence against their own need and their disquiet that desire ends in an extinction of self. The presence of autonomous, desiring women would threaten men's vulnerability and undermine the fantasy of men's sexual omnipotence. And yet the participation of other men in a man's sexual fantasy betrays his homoeroticism. The anonymous strangers fucking his wife are the type of men he wants to emulate – fucking an anonymous woman while her husband watches. It is the ultimate and longed for moment of domination.

It is an apocryphal moment. As the husband watches and dreams of being omnipotent like these strangers, he is no more than a voyeur, a masochist peeking at the scene of his own punishment. The sexual thrill is to be humiliated and dominated by other men. In these scenarios women's bodies are merely the objects for the exchange of pleasure between men. 'Harry of Barnstable' watched his wife as 'One of the other men got down in front of [her] and waved his cock in front of her face.' In this fantasy, who does he pretend to be – his wife or the man? 'My heart missed a beat as I watched her kiss and suck the stranger's cock as Bill fucked her.'

How many straight men envy the stereotyped sexual culture of gay men: cruising, cottaging, the thrill of the chance encounter? This is a masculine fantasy of pure sex, an activity only available to heterosexual men in a limited form through the cash nexus of prostitution and the fantasies of pornography. But the ephemeral seductions of gay men are not a simple mimicry of straight male promiscuity. Anonymous gay sex avoids intimacy, but it is also a contract of depersonalized desire agreed by both parties. In this respect it carries the possibility of different forms of togetherness, not open to heterosexual men in their relationships with women.

For some men the answer to the problems of male desire is to renounce it. John Stoltenburg has argued that pornography is the expression of male violence against women: 'Your penis is a weapon, her body is your target. And pornography says about that sexuality . . . men are masters and women are slaves . . . men are sex machines women are sluts.' The journalist Peter Baker calls for a new model of male heterosexuality to replace the aggression and emotional failings of the old: 'Tender men . . . are more interested in closeness and cuddles than copulation. They prefer to kiss and pet for hours than come in minutes.' For both men, eroticism is reduced to its nice, 'soft' components. Sex must be rid of its objectifying lust and its fantasies. They argue that a man needs to create a union with his lover in which he can completely know and experience her. The problem with this vision of sexuality is that our desire can never be permanently fixed in the body of one other individual, nor can it be for ever confined to an intimate relationship with one other person. Desire transgresses boundaries. It upsets the order of things. By its nature, whether in fantasy or reality, it betrays the fidelity of relationships. What turns us on are images, strangers, objects, associations. Even the monotonous fantasies of men's pornography reveal a more complex story of male desire than straightforward lust for women's bodies.

Men's sexuality has traditionally been based on the assumption that 'good' women were not interested in sex – or at least that they shouldn't be. Women are now asserting their own sexuality, challenging the way in which men have divorced sex from love. The furore in the British press in June 1995 when Hugh Grant was caught with a prostitute in Los Angeles and charged with 'lewd conduct' shattered the aura of romantic love which surrounded him.' What will the girl with the prettiest boyfriend in Britain decide to do?' asked Jane Green in the *Daily Express*. 'Certainly she will scream "How could you, Hugh?" ' Real life met

Seduction

fiction in that familiar male conflict between sex and love. The following year the media interest in the BBC drama *Pride and Prejudice* singled out the manly character of Darcy. Countless vox pops and articles appeared in the press eulogizing his sexual allure. The interest reflected a longing for a mythical past in which male sexual virility did not negate love; a desire for men to be both erotic and constant in their attentions. The gaze of Darcy as it falls upon his beloved is an event which is rare in contemporary culture, a sublime moment of erotic desire which is also a moment of love. It is this reordering of the boundaries between sex and love, between emotion and desire that concerns men.

IV

What could expose men's vulnerability more than being in love? Opening up to a woman, relinquishing control and trusting her. Men come and they go, flitting in and out of the web of their need of women.

I spent the last two years of my life in Southampton employed in a small co-operative which leased a couple of lorries to make door-to-door collections of household waste paper. I drove one of the lorries with a friend W. She was a couple of years older than me and had recently separated from her husband. She had given birth to her son in a caravan in the Welsh countryside, where she spent his first year going mad with loneliness and boredom. She enjoyed city life and had rejected her husband's hippy privations.

She wanted love, but she guarded herself against men. I can no longer remember where we met – I think it was at C's house. We'd known each other for several years and for some time we went out together every Friday night. One Friday W had made a special meal and invited me to her house instead. It was her way of saying she wanted a relationship with me. I pretended not to hear her: I wanted us to remain friends.

I can remember my last Friday morning at work. The following week I was leaving Southampton to live in London. It was twenty past nine when W drove the lorry out of the depot. The rain had stopped and the first, warm light from the sun had broken through the cloud. Everywhere was wet and reflected a dazzling brightness. She drove out of the industrial estate and onto the dual carriageway heading for the university side of town. I was flicking through the newspaper and my attention was caught by an article in the business section. A large multinational company had announced its decision to close its British paper mill. I pointed out the article and W said: 'I don't think we can survive for much longer.' I said: 'I'm leaving at the right time.' I regretted my lack of tact and apologized. 'Yea,' acknowledged W, 'and I suppose I'll be back on Social Security.' It was 1979 and a period of my life was coming to an end. I glanced at W as she concentrated on the road ahead. I remembered the meal she had made six months earlier, sitting on an old mattress in her living room, eating an avocado pear. I tried to imagine how things would have been if we had become lovers and set up house together, and I knew it wouldn't have worked. As the reflecting light brimmed across the road ahead of us I thought about how I would say goodbye to W.

When I did say goodbye to her, it was a perfunctory goodbye. It failed to convey the value of our friendship. It was my evasion. I left. I travelled up to London in a van to the room recently vacated by my friend. I travelled up with F, who helped me unload my possessions and then returned to Southampton. It was like going on holiday and then discovering myself alone and the anticipation soured.

Several weeks later I had a letter from F, who wanted to come and stay with me. I was unsure; she took the initiative. I agreed and arranged to meet her in the market in Covent Garden. She took the coach to London and arrived on Saturday evening. It was winter, and it had begun to snow. I waited for her, leaning against the railings looking down on the empty benches where, in warmer weather, people sat drinking after work. I saw her and waved as she crossed over to me. She was wearing a fake fur coat and heavy boots and her hair was cropped short. She was with a group of women she had travelled with. They said goodbye to her and I, nervous, looked at her as if looking at someone for the first time. 'How was the journey?' I asked. 'Fine.' I suggested we go for a drink, but she preferred to go back to my place. We slept together in the small single bed. The following day it was still snowing. We got up late and walked several miles to Hampstead Heath, which looked white and blasted in the snow. Our feet left a trail of prints. We walked to the cinema in Hampstead and watched a film called *Zéro de Conduite* and then went to a pub, where I won £2 on a fruit machine. We walked back home and two days later F returned home and my days, which had been full, now seemed familiar again, and empty.

We wrote to each other and F came down again the following month. In May she left her own house and moved in – temporarily to begin with and then permanently. I was unable to leave, even though I tried to on a number of occasions in that first year. Not literally; I evaded her by retreating into myself – I couldn't manage the closeness. And then, in Chichester, watching its skyline, I was in love with F; a slow, uneven and difficult falling in love. That was eighteen years ago. And now I am reminded of the Masonic Hall and myself at thirteen, dancing to Mrs R's old-fashioned tunes with K, my first encounter with love, a friend who I also desired, and who I also never said goodbye to.

7

LOVE

And our faces, my heart, brief as photos.

JOHN BERGER

I

I had been sorting through a cupboard and an old photograph of my father's mother fell out of an envelope. It is sepia and faded and must be eighty years old. It was taken in a small back yard and shows her as a young girl, about fourteen years of age, wearing a sun hat and sitting in a deck chair next to a rather morose old woman, who is knitting. My grandmother has a beautiful face and she has lifted her eyes from the embroidery on her lap, and is staring directly into the camera. I wonder who it is she is looking at, because there is a wistful expression in her eyes. She is dead now, but here in this picture and in her rather melancholy gaze her whole life awaited her. When I think about love I am drawn to the thought of death.. I am not particularly morbid, but when we love someone, when our own life becomes integral to their life, then we necessarily face the prospect of mortality. Love is the great risk we take in life; we have to make the choice to surrender ourselves to it and so must be prepared for its loss. To be able to love, we must be able to mourn.

Last night I woke after a particularly disturbing dream. I had been with F, somewhere vague and diffuse. A woman approached us and asked if we would like our fortunes read. 'Why not?' I said. As I spoke, two sheets of paper appeared, pinned to some kind of monorail. Each had writing on its reverse side, and it was only possible to read the print backwards through the thin paper. As they approached us I tried to read them and noticed, to my horror, that they revealed the age at which each of us would die. I attempted to stop the woman. I told her I didn't want this kind of knowledge. She apologized and said that once she had begun her prediction, it was not possible to halt it. While F would live into relative old age, I would die in a matter of a few years. I woke and felt an intense sense of relief that it had been only a dream. Then I began to imagine that the dream itself might be prophetic and that I would die soon. I felt a terrible foreboding. Even now I cannot bring myself to write down the ages written on those pieces of paper.

On Saturday 6 September 1997 I walked onto Horse Guards Parade with my son. Thousands of people sat both alone and in groups, listening to 'Libera me', an aria from Verdi's *Requiem*. Loudspeakers had been installed at strategic points around Westminster Abbey, and the melancholy sound of the soprano's voice lifted and swam across the open space. It felt as if the whole of London was still, contemplating in silence the loss of something intangible yet crucial to our identities. During that bizarre and disturbing week of national mourning for the death of Diana, Princess of Wales, I found my republican disdain undermined by my own feelings of loss. I was shocked by the news of her death, but I was determined not to capitulate to the media-generated delirium. I had avoided television and the press during the royal wedding and I intended to do so again. As the week progressed I found it harder to contain my feelings. By Wednesday I had succumbed and took the tube into central London. Wandering around Kensington Palace and then down through Hyde Park to Buckingham Palace and the Mall was a type of minor pilgrimage. A population had been mobilized in an unprecedented display of public grief. The letters of condolence, messages of empathy and whimsical poems of bereavement reiterated the word 'love'. As I watched the crowds arriving to pay their respects it seemed as if the country – the southern part at least – had been overwhelmed by a feudal deference to royalty. We were all peasants again, a mob whose reason had been suspended by our need to express our feelings of loss.

What was it we were mourning? Our own dead mothers, fathers and grandparents? The loss of a sense of national identity? Or was the emotional religiosity an inexplicable grief for ourselves? Standing in the square on the day of Diana's funeral I imagined this extraordinary spectacle might signal a release from our national equivocation with the past. She personified a national desire to become a vibrant, modern and fairer society which valued individuals and their feelings. But she was a profoundly ambiguous figure compromised by her wealth and by her own need for social status. As I waited with the crowds on the Mall for the funeral procession, expecting the pomp and circumstance of a parade of cars, even a mounted guard, I was caught unawares by the single hearse that glided silently past. Was this the long deferential relationship of the people to the monarchy passing into history? In the traffic-free serenity of London, I felt a sense of liberation, as if, for a fleeting moment, the crowds were mourning the passing of an old order and had taken possession of their own city. I thought of my mother, her vacillation between freedom and security and my own irresolute love for her. We all live in a liminal state between loss and love, between the old and the new, between desire and need. Diana became the embodiment of this modern condition: she represented not love, but a search for love.

The day my mother died I was visiting the National Gallery in London. At the time she lay alone and unconscious on her bed I was standing in front of a painting by Titian, the guide praising the quality of the brushwork. I had grown restless during the tour and my mind was on the quickest route to the café in the basement. As soon as the guide had completed her talk I walked down the stairs. The café was crowded, but I found a table occupied by a solitary older woman. I asked if I could sit down and she gestured to a spare seat. I bought myself a pot of tea. I lifted the tea bag out of the pot, poured myself a cup and sat for a while, thinking of nothing. Someone had left a newspaper on a chair and I picked it up and skimmed through it. The woman took a handkerchief out of her shopping bag and demurely wiped the cake crumbs from her mouth. Then she rose, gave me a slight nod, and left. And then I too left and walked out into the autumn afternoon. The sun was shining across Trafalgar Square which, although it was October, was still crowded with tourists. I walked up Charing Cross Road to Oxford Street and caught the bus home.

My mother was my first love. I loved her, or rather I wanted to love her, more than was reasonable. And when I grew older she brought my first disappointment, my first bereavement when I learnt that I could not have the reverie of her love and her body. I was unable to mourn this. I continued to wait for her to recognize my plight and for the enchanting moment when she would give me her life. In adolescence I hovered uneasily around her, resentful and unable to tear myself away. I would soar out of her reach, only to plummet to earth when I was unable to sustain the intensity of my flight. I carried this childish and selfish yearning for my own freedom into adulthood. But in her death I began to mourn my loss of her. I sat by her coffin in a nondescript room at the undertaker's. Her hair had been washed in a cheap shampoo which had stripped away the natural oils and it lay on the nylon pillow like a shapeless heap of flax. I tried to smooth it around her face, but each individual strand of hair was infused with static, and the more I patted them the more unruly they became. The back of her head had been sawn off in the autopsy and her face was distorted, her lips, nose and cheek bones flattened. I imagined her body, beneath the dress we had chosen for her, butchered and sewn. When we were children she never hid her body from us. Now the skin on her face, forearms and hands was cold and hardening. I wanted to get up from the chair and walk out of the small bare room, but I could not bring myself to move. I would sit motionless and wait, if necessary for ever, while she lay still and placid. I mustered my composure and called down the corridor for F. When she walked in I told her I couldn't leave. I asked her to help me leave. She came and stood next to me and then I stood up and said goodbye.

I think men's difficulties in loving women lie in our difficulties in mourning. Masculinity is built on losses, and it sustains itself by refusing to countenance them. Caught in this conundrum we oscillate between the adolescent illusion of omnipotence and a despair at the limits of our own existence. We blame women for holding us back, for entrapping and enticing and stifling us. We accuse them of being the source of our pain and bewilderment. T. S. Eliot in his play *The Cocktail Party* poignantly depicts the inability to mourn the loss of love. In the second act Edward Chamberlayne, whose marriage is collapsing, seeks the help of a psychiatrist, Sir Henry Harcourt-Reilly. He tells the doctor that he wants to be placed in a sanatorium: he is ill in a way he cannot explain. He confesses:

I see now why I wanted my wife to come back.
It was because of what she had made me into . . .
When I thought she had left me, I began to dissolve,
To cease to exist. That was what she had done to me!
I cannot live with her – that is now intolerable;
I cannot live without her, for she has made me incapable
Of having an existence of my own.

Unable to mourn the loss of his wife's love, he is a man
who no longer knows his own mind. He denies the value
of his own life and clutches at her absence. She alternates
between a maternal icon who will assuage his need and an
avenging temptress set upon destroying him. He subsides
in a state of non-existence. It is the little deaths men fear
from their need of women. And it is to our fathers who
symbolize our future and our desire, that we turn for help.

II

In the summer of 1945, when he was eighteen years old,
my father joined the army. The following year he was com-
missioned as a second lieutenant and sent abroad to Trieste,
where he found himself on the wrong side of the border
with the former Yugoslavia and was locked in a gaol for
the night. He was involved in the policing of Palestine, and
took part in the campaign against the communist insurgents
in Malaya. He was a young man at the end of an era, when
Britain's imperial culture was collapsing. Its impact on his
life was lessened by a military regime governed by tradition,
regularity and imposed discipline. His transition to adulthood followed the well-defined protocols of its masculine
world. He knew his duty and his responsibilities, and
belonged to an organization which prided itself on its strong
social cohesion. When he left the army in 1948, he found
a position in a firm in the City, where he remained for the
whole of his working life. Like other men of the period,
my father did not question what it meant to be a husband

and father. That would have been to state the obvious. He inhabited the institutions of the army, work and marriage as the purveyor of their order. Perhaps I exaggerate the degree of conventionality. The war had taken its toll on family life. Children had grown up without fathers, husbands had been separated from their wives and children, and women were coming to terms with the loss of their wartime jobs and independence. Nevertheless the 1950s have become a nostalgic emblem of a social order which was governed by shared, common-sense assumptions about the 'normal' roles of men and women; a period when the middle-class family was secure.

When I was the same age as my father had been in the army, bound by the dictates of authority, I was interested in the ideas of the women's movement. In one generation, within the same family, my father and I were contemplating a rapidly changing world in markedly different ways. There was almost no common language between us. The influential social commentator Francis Fukuyama has called this extreme discontinuity of fatherhood and family life the 'Great Disruption'. He is afraid that fathers have lost their authority over their sons, which he believes will lead to the breakdown of the family and an increase in poverty, child abuse and educational underachievement. Without a proper moral order, men will no longer feel the obligation to stay with their wives and children. His solution is to return us to our traditional roles. The authority of the father must be restored. Men must once again become the main bread-winner of their families and women must care for the children. His ideas are shared by the journalist Melanie Phillips,

who wrote in the *Observer*: 'Breadwinning is essential for
male identity in a way it is not for the vast majority of
mothers.' She argues that women's increased equality has
led to a contempt for men and a 'female supremacism',
which is responsible for men's 'growing rage'.

The changes in the relationships between men and women
are like tectonic plates shifting beneath the earth's crust.
Almost imperceptible, their effect on our lives is nevertheless dramatic and far reaching. What do we do about them?
There are those, like Francis Fukuyama and Melanie Phillips, who can see only disaster ahead and want to recover
the vestiges of the old order. For them the sexual liberation
movements of the 1960s and 1970s were harbingers of
social chaos, peopled by individuals unable to accept the
conventions of everyday life. They want to rebuild the traditional roles of men and women – 'A man's job is to win
the bread. A woman's to spread it.' I can understand their
anxieties but I do not agree with their solutions. We cannot
simply turn the clock back. In any case, there never was a
golden age in which the family was secure and men and
women were content with their stations in life. The sexual
liberation movements were a revolt against an old order and
morality too rigid to accept the new emotions, identities
and aspirations of people living in a changing world. New
forms of family life have been created: lesbian mothers, gay
fathers, women on their own with children, family groups
without children whose ties are friendship or affiliation to
a lifestyle. The traditional figure of the father has lost his
power and this has precipitated uncertainty and confusion,
but few want a return to the past when those who flouted

convention were cast to the margins. His demise has allowed a more tolerant society to develop and helped to emancipate women and gay men. The impact upon many heterosexual men has been more ambiguous because for them these changes represent a loss. The father who once personified their future birthright and who promised recompense for the loss of their mothers' love is in decline.

In recent years we have been inundated with pop stars, politicians and personalities who improve their image by being photographed with their children. The idea that fatherhood is a fashion statement does little to resolve the problems men face in relationships. There are still precious few role models of men who are respected because of their emotional resilience and empathy, rather than their domineering behaviour. *The Full Monty* was one of the most popular films of 1997. Robert Carlyle played Gaz, an unemployed steelworker, struggling to support such a persona against a world turned upside-down. Gaz personifies the predicament of men as he attempts to find a balance between self-validating displays of toughness and a greater sensitivity and concern for others. When he performs his striptease to the sound of Hot Chocolate's 'You Sexy Thing', he offers us the image of a male sexuality which isn't about goals or about the acquisition of women, but about the body and pleasure. Part of the film's enormous appeal lies in Gaz's subversion of the traditional male stereotype. He is as yet something of an exception; men are portrayed more frequently as weak, untrustworthy or despicable characters who cannot be depended upon.

In advertising, men in the home are frequently portrayed

as bumbling clowns struggling to use a washing machine, or engaged in a botched attempt to look after the children. In the mid 1980s Kitty O'Hagen, a planning director at the ad company GGK, researched women's opinions of the portrayal of women in advertising. She found that women were deeply dissatisfied with the depiction of both men and women in adverts: 'Where are the men doing household chores? More men do them now, but it's like a closet activity they don't admit to. Women want to be represented as independent and resourceful individuals. Men must want something different too!' A decade later, in 1995, Lucy Banister, an associate director of Davies Riley-Smith, produced a report 'The Best a Man Can Get?', which found men increasingly anxious about the portrayal of their bodies as sex objects. Adverts promoting female authority 'confirmed the pressure [men] were feeling from other sources, both at work and socially'. In 1998 marketing consultants Mellors Reay and Partners published *The State of Men*, which found that men are attracted to images of masculinity which have an aura of the macho, elemental and rugged. Men feel they no longer possess these qualities and advertisers need to appeal to their fantasies of being a warrior and hero. The report claimed that we are 'a nation of mummy's boys failing to leave home'. In 1991 one in eleven thirty-to-thirty-four-year-old men were still living with their parents. By 1996 the figure had risen to one in nine. While men have become more dependent, women have been gaining independence and establishing networks of friends.

Some men feel deeply aggrieved about what is happening to them. In their minds the most glaring injustice is the exclusion of separated and divorced fathers from their own children. Acrimonious disputes over custody have encouraged the search for a scapegoat in feminism. David Thomas in *Not Guilty: In Defence of Modern Man* argues: 'Whichever way you roll the dice, the game of parenthood is more viciously loaded against men than the meanest crap shoot in Vegas.' Groups like Families Need Fathers and the UK Men's Movement present men as victims of feminism and compound the advertising images of hopeless men burning the tea. The vehemence with which some men loathe feminism comes from their perception of female power in domestic and private life. The emotional dexterity women have used to manage family relationships is now increasingly valued in work. Women's ways of thinking and doing things are no longer confined to the home and men often feel threatened and unwanted. Men carry into adult life a need for love and security from women which they find difficult to reciprocate. Dependency leads men to distance themselves from their own feelings of need, and creates the kind of insensitivity, narcissism and macho displays everyone is familiar with. At one time men could be emotionally demanding at home and macho in public, but now women are less prepared to put up with this type of masculinity. Men are increasingly trapped between their old, unacceptable behaviour and a discomforting personal vulnerability.

Men are caught between the old and the new and there appears to be no father figure to set them an example. In some respects patrimony – that which a father hands down to his children – has been turned on its head. It is no longer just what a father can give to his son, but what a son might give to his father. The popular metaphor of the 'inner child' encourages the idea that it is in the boy that he once was that a man can discover the origins of himself. Men who wish to be close to their sons can find a means of recovering emotions repudiated in their own youth. Such identification can lead to confusion between feelings that should belong to sons and feelings that should belong to fathers. The collapse of paternal authority has encouraged men to escape being mother's boys by joining their sons in a rebellious camaraderie against her. I think this is part of the fear expressed by Francis Fukuyama and Melanie Phillips. They perceive that men are either uninterested in their children or New Man types unable to provide the stability and constancy of adult authority, because, like adolescents, they are caught in the same perplexing state between childhood and adulthood.

We no longer live in a patriarchal society in which men hold sway. We live with the legacies of such a society. We don't know what will take its place, but it has gone and will never come back and men have to give up their emotional investment in it. This does not mean accepting injustices done to individual men, nor does it mean giving way to women. There is a world to be gained from men's loss of patriarchal authority. The muddle and confusion is something to be lived with while we come to terms with the loss of the old.

In his short story *Where He Was: Memories of My Father* Raymond Carver describes a man who drank, became depressed and suffered poverty. Father and son shared the same first name and the same problem with alcohol. When his father died, Carver kept a photograph of him on his wall. Every now and then he'd look at the picture and try and fathom something about his father, and in the process about himself. But he couldn't. His father kept receding back into time, and then he lost the picture. After his father's funeral he thought that he would remember everything that had happened that day. But except for one memory he had forgotten it all: 'What I do remember is that I heard our name used a lot that afternoon, my dad's name and mine. But I knew they were talking about my dad. *Raymond*, these people kept saying in their beautiful voices out of my childhood. *Raymond*.'

There is something wistful about Carver's story. It is without hope, as if memories of loss will always inter us in the past. In contrast to this, I am reminded of Rachel Whiteread's sculpture, *Ghost*, a large plaster cast of the interior of a room from a Victorian house. In its evocation of a bygone world it similarly calls on the memories of our childhoods and our mothers and fathers. The fossilized adornments of this anonymous room confront us with absence and silence, but unlike Carver's story, they invite us to make something of them. The past is there for us to use and to change; to discover in what direction we should go. *Ghost* symbolizes the state we are in, a tentative moving beyond ourselves, the search for a new language of love and relationships.

II

When I try to talk about love, I can find words, but they are without syntax and grammar, and so they have no meaning. I'm still not certain I know what love is. There are no sentences which will describe something we cannot conceive of. In his poem 'East Coker' T. S. Eliot describes his unending quest for meaning. He strives to express what he wants to say. A venture into language must be undertaken, and a new beginning made, 'a raid on the inarticulate', an attempt to put into words the 'imprecision of feeling' and the 'undisciplined squads of emotion'.

> There is only the fight to recover what has been lost
> And found and lost again and again: and now, under
>   conditions
> That seem unpropitious. But perhaps neither gain nor
>   loss.
> For us, there is only the trying. The rest is not our
>   business.

Men use language as an instrument to change the world and to demonstrate and confirm our own individuality and separateness from others. We want to know the facts, uncover empirical truths, name, classify and grade objects. We exile ourselves in language. Eliot shows us another way of using it. He abandons philosophical certainties and clearly defined goals – 'For us, there is only the trying.'

I am back where I started. I need to find a vocabulary of love, a language of exploration. My first thought is walking.

It has its own rhetoric of ambling, drifting, straying, strolling, hiking. I walk in order to know the places and the buildings I pass and in order to find out about myself. I walk in order to think. I walk out of my street up to the more suburban, residential roads. I follow familiar routes and repeat them countless times and I am never bored by their ordinariness: the Victorian railway bridge with its thirty-year-old anti-Vietnam War graffiti; the underground reservoir and its acres of unpopulated green. I walk up the hill alongside its flaking metal fencing and at the end of the road I turn right and pass down my favourite stretch of road, which in spring is lined with the pink blossom of the cherry trees and in summer is a haze of dark, shaded green, overhung by the row of giant plane trees which border the top end of the reservoir. I'm up high here, and can look across London to Canary Wharf and beyond to the low hills on the far side of south-east London. Everything appears absolutely still: the dome of St Paul's, the four chimneys of Battersea power station, the tall, spiky cluster of the City, the Shell building on the South Bank, Parliament. If I am here at dusk I am surrounded by darkness while the city is crowned in lights. Then I walk down the hill and turn right, and then left and right again and I follow the road round to the high street and the rows of shops and Woolworths opposite. If there's time I browse in the bookshop and buy bread, vegetables, fruit. When I have finished shopping I walk home. In good weather I walk down the road past the playing fields which stretch across to a row of tall poplars, and then take a long circuitous route back home. But in winter I return as the crow would fly, along the high street and up the hill, with its constant line of traffic, and then down, over the disused railway line, out of the suburban green and into the closed streets of the city, with their scuff of dirt and grey, home to the terraced row and the small park opposite.

In my walking from home back to home, everything is here, even what is beyond my understanding. It is in our natures to reach for this something more which is beyond us. It is our determination to *know*, to grasp for words which will correspond to what is missing. Words rise to the surface, like bubbles of air rise in water. They reach the surface and disperse into me. And what comes to mind are the lines from a poem by O. V. de Milosz called 'Melancholy': 'I say Mother. And my thoughts are of you, oh, House. / House of the lovely dark summers of my childhood.' And I know that throughout my life I will live partly in this place. All of us do. The house is a symbol of our own self and the integrity of our boundaries. Here we descend to excavate our dreams; here is the tomb in which we will be laid after our death, and the place where we were born. It is here that our lives began and we formed our first words. And what we men must understand is that it belongs to a woman, and that our masculinity has exiled us from it. In our desire to live, there remains our need. The two are interdependent.

The Estonian poet Jaan Kaplinski wrote about being alone in his house after his wife and children had left for a short holiday. At first he is afraid. Then his mind wanders and he daydreams of embarking on an adventure unencumbered by a wife and children. Finally, he decides on a more prosaic response to their absence:

simply dive
into this silence of home space-time,
flow with this murky winter day
and in this flowing rediscover
window, door, walls, ceiling, shadows and light,
my own body and my absent wife and children
somewhere in the same time in the light of the same
winter day.

It is here in silence, in this 'same winter day', that a language of men's love for women is to be made. What will we find there? The answer is nothing. After all the effort to reach this moment, what an irony! But something does exist which is other than simply nothing, and that is an absence. An absence of words with which to describe men's original state of dependency on our mothers; the fear of being lost and abandoned by them; the moment of loss when time is frozen and language recedes. This is the nature of our bodies without women – bereft; much the same still as the nature of our childhood bodies without our mothers. Love does not emerge out of the silence, like Aphrodite from the sea. It has to be created. Silence is not emptiness. It is feeling that is waiting for words.

And all I can think to say is that this is no conclusion, because there isn't one, merely a beginning, and I know you are waiting, not because I can't love you but because I don't know how I might say that in you I've learnt to live. Perhaps what I am trying to say is that I never became myself until I loved you. And then. For all the words I've written on this paper, I'm still trying to find my tongue.

ACKNOWLEDGEMENTS

I'd like to thank Janet Harbord and Frances Angela for reading drafts of the typescript and for providing me with their insights and critical comments.

The Author and Publishers have made every effort to trace all copyright holders of quoted materials and apologise for any ommissions. The Publishers are happy to receive any emendations from copyright holders.

The Author and Publishers are grateful to the proprietors listed below for permission to quote from the following material: excerpts from *The Cocktail Party* and 'East Coke' from T S Eliot's *The Complete Poems and Plays* © the estate of T S Eliot and Faber & Faber; an extract from *Big Sur* by Jack Kerouac © the estate of Jack Kerouac and André Deutsch Ltd; an extract from 'The Children are away from home' from *Through the Forest* by Jaan Kaplinski, translated by Hildi Hawkins © Jaan Kaplinski and Harvill Press; an extract from 'Blackbird Pie' from *Elephant and*

I Am No Longer Myself Without You